KEEP SMILING THROUGH

Second World War
Letters from Prisoner of War Camps

Best wishes

Sandra Delf

Copyright © Sandra Delf 2016

Published by East Anglian Press

British Library Cataloguing in Publication Data.

A CIP catalogue record for this book is available from the British Library.

ISBN-13: 978-0-9954844-0-5

Acknowledgements:

I would like to thank the following for their help and support.

My brother, Roger Evans

My husband, Jack Delf

Ivan Bunn, local historian, for his maps

Ian Robb, local historian

Jill Powell and the Lowestoft U3A Writers Group

Suzan Collins and the Waveney Author Group

Janis Kirby and the Lowestoft U3A Family History Group

Malcolm Tudor, who allowed me to quote from his book "British Prisoners of War in Italy: Paths to Freedom".

Peter Doyle, who allowed me to quote from his book "Prisoner of War in Germany".

The Alexander Turnbull Library, National Library of New Zealand for permission to use the front cover photograph.

The National Ex-Prisoner of War Association.

Contents

INTRODUCTION

Over 200,000 soldiers of the British armed forces were captured during the Second World War. The extracts of letters contained in this book were written from North Africa, and Prisoner of War camps in Italy and Germany. They run from January 1941 to May 1945 and were written by my father Cyril Evans.

Cyril was born in Payne Street, Kirkley, Lowestoft in 1905 and attended the Central School there. After joining the Borough Surveyor's Department at Lowestoft Borough Council in May 1921 he moved to the Costing Department in 1937.

By the time WW2 broke out he was married and living in Walmer Road, Pakefield. This house was commandeered by the army, so his wife, 'Kathleen', went to live with her mother for the duration of the war. For this reason some of the letters and official documents were sent to an address in Beaconsfield Road, Lowestoft.

Cyril was a Sergeant in the Royal Ordnance Corps with the 3rd Armoured Brigade in North Africa when, in 1941, he was captured. An eyewitness report of his capture, taken from the

War Diary of H.Q. 3rd Armoured Brigade, is included.

Most of Cyril's letter and postcard allowance was sent to his wife and she passed them on to the rest of the family. Before he went to war, Cyril and Kathleen agreed that each would note the date, each month, they first saw the new moon. They would then compare this date in their letters hoping it would prove they had been looking at the new moon at about the same time. For this reason many of Cyril's letters reported the date he saw the new moon; I have left some of these references in.

The letters describe one man's experience of being a prisoner of war and show a preoccupation with food, Red Cross Parcels and mail from home. With very few exceptions his letters convey a probably "over positive" mood.

> "… letters sent home give the idea of a life rosier than it really is…Complaining letters are few, men who feel downhearted do not mention it."[1]

Although Cyril's letters have been edited the words he used are unchanged and the language is

---

[1] Source: 'Prisoner of War', a leaflet published by the Red Cross in 1942, page 11.

'of the time'. The letters are a witness to prices, wages and tax details. They also show his constant looking forward, optimism, how he dealt with the boredom and his gradual institutionalisation. There are also details of how he and his companions made their food go further and the conditions they endured.

Many, but not all, prisoners completed Questionnaires / Interrogation Reports after the war. No Liberation/Interrogation Report was found for Cyril at the National Archives

Although Cyril heard those, now, well known words, 'For you the war is over,' from his captors, it was not. It was the start of a new battle. For him, and his companions, it went on in the form of a lack of freedom, crushing boredom, humiliation, overcrowding and hunger.[2]

They endured the bitter Italian winter of 1941 – 2 when no Red Cross parcels arrived.

---

[2] ....the men received half a kilo of bread a day. The other staple issue was 120 grammes of either rice or low-grade macaroni daily. For five days of the week they got 40 grammes of cheese. On the other two days it was 40 grammes of meat, which included such delicacies as cows' udder and lung. The 40 grammes included bone and gristle of which it largely consisted. Source: 'Give Me Air', Edward Ward page 46

In isolation from the rest of the world they suffered an environment of armed guards, barbed wire, searchlights, squalid conditions and guard dogs.

Cyril's experience of being a POW was not as harsh as those in the Far East and under article 27 of the Geneva Convention, Officers and senior NCOs were exempt from working, therefore, Cyril was not in a 'working camp'.

Keeping the POWs hungry, however, was a deliberate policy as it diminished their morale. Most of their food came from Red Cross parcels which were, of course, supposed to only supplement their rations. The contents of the Red Cross Parcels were cooked by the POWs themselves who had to improvise with their methods.

Unlike a criminal, who has a sentence passed down, for the POWs their sentence was of unknown length. Those at home wondered whether *their* POW would survive.

Sandra Delf

Cyril with Kathleen before the war.

KRIEGIE THOUGHTS

Barbed Wire! Barbed Wire! Barbed Wire!
To the North, South, West and East
Will it always hold me captive?
Without hope or joy or peace

Must I ever curve this eager flame?
That burns within my chest
Or know once more the joy of home
With pleasant hours of rest

Such questions to my mind do crowd
When deep in thought I sit
But ever with it comes the cry
It won't be long don't quit

And so it goes from day to day
A never changing scene
But someday soon I will leave it all
As though it were a dream.

Author Unknown

'Kriegie' - what POWs called themselves. It is short for
Kriegesgefangenen, which is the German word for
Prisoner of war.

11

Cyril at home at the beginning of the war.

Cyril bottom left. Others unknown.

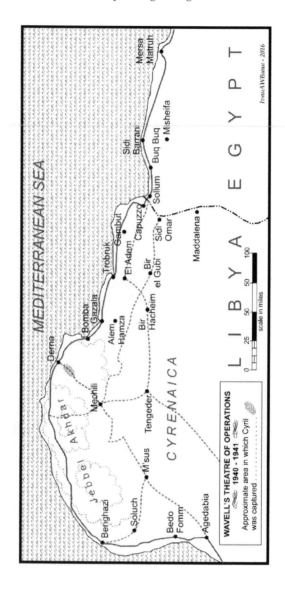

CAMPO 78

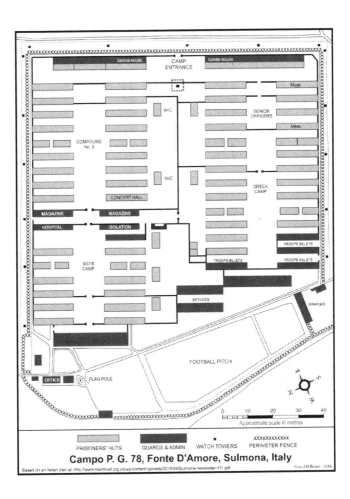

Campo P. G. 78, Fonte D'Amore, Sulmona, Italy

BEFORE CAPTURE – NORTH AFRICA

Cyril was a Sergeant with Royal Army Ordnance Corps attached to 3rd Armoured Brigade.

After being evacuated from Dunkirk he embarked for the Middle East on 30th October 1940. He was with the 3rd Armoured Brigade during the North African Campaign and took part in the withdrawal from western Cyrenaica, a province of Italian Libya.

We start with a letter from Egypt.

Sent from 3rd Armoured Brigade, O.F.P[3] Section c/o Army Post Office 727, 4th January 1941.

"At last my mail has arrived – the letter you wrote on Oct 30th and one from the Borough Treasurer. Mr. Robertson sent me a statement as follows.

Gross Civilian Salary				**18 6 8**
Less Army pay (31 days at 6/3)	9	13	9	
Wife's allowance 17/- x 52	3	13	8	
12				
Superannuation		18	4	
Rates	1	0	0	<u>15 5 9</u>
Money order sent				£3 0 11

---

[3] Ordnance Field Park.

A strong wind was blowing during the early part of the week and meal-times were rather unpleasant. The nights too were very cold. The last few days have been warmer and today we are back to shirts and shorts after being glad to wear battle dress earlier in the week.

I went to the pictures on New Year's Eve and saw one of our old favourites "Winterset". The guard woke us that night at midnight and I went outside the tent with one or two others. I felt far away from home. The guard woke me again when it was midnight at home and I drank your health. Not in champagne this year, but in Moya – which is water."

I saw the new moon as I was going to the pictures at 5.30 on New Year's Eve. I was with Bill Challis that evening and after the show we walked down to the NAAFI. On the way we met two Aussies and we had supper with them, eggs and chips. They knew we had just come out and wanted to know all about the air-raids. They think the people at home are wonderful and so do we.

Sunday Evening

"I am just back from the cinema, where I saw Robert Montgomery and Rosalind Russell in "Live, Love and Learn". Just as the main film started the camera broke down and during the wait someone shouted "Give it to the Spitfire Fund", and later there was a "ssh!" followed by a loud cheer.

I am writing this on a packing case by the light of a hurricane lamp. We have a Stores Tent now where we sort out our wares, and I sleep in here with "Buff". We have to go back to the tent we left behind to hear the radio. This war is going very well for us now and I expect it will be better still when this arrives.[4] I've just remembered something else that happened as we were leaving camp in England. After the march, as I sat there, my watch dropped off my wrist on to my lap. The clip couldn't have been fastened properly. It was strange that it hadn't dropped off during the march. I should have lost it then for sure.

---

[4] In January 1941 Australian troops assaulted the Italian stronghold in Libya, taking 5,000 prisoners. The Allies captured 25,000 Italians. This would explain Cyril's comment about the war going well.

We are lucky to have a cinema and **NAAFI** so near. The natives often drive herds of goats or sheep by here, but it is a mystery what the animals find to eat. Our washing is done quite well by the natives for ½ **PT.** ($1^{1/4d}$) an article."

Sent from 3rd Armoured Brigade, O.F.P Section C, 12th January 1941.

"This letter will be blotted by the old fashioned method of dusting with sand. In other words, we are having a sand storm. Although this tent is well put up and lined inside with cases of stores there is a yellow haze inside and a layer of dust everywhere. Outside, it is hard to see the next tent and during heavy gusts of wind, impossible to see anything. Breakfast was a bit gritty but very good, oats, and boiled egg and tinned bacon on bread.

I see that the stamps put on these letters show we are in Egypt. So I might have said so before. I'm not so far away after all, although it took eight weeks to get here.

"We had a surprise on Friday. We were going into town for a bath in the morning and we were told we could stay all day.

It was about 10.30am when we arrived. The baths were at one of the Service Clubs. We spent nearly an hour in a bookshop looking at the stock. There were two Zane Grey books there, but they were too dear, about 3/- each with paper covers. From there we went along to the sea-front, a very nice bay with a duel carriageway road and tall buildings – but no beach.

We had a chicken sandwich and coffee and after that went to look for a cinema. Cyril and I decided to see John Garfield and Ann Sheridan in 'Castle on the Hudson'.

Our cinema was about the size of the 'Palace' (a Lowestoft cinema), and as usual out here, all the seats were wicker arm-chairs. We went in the cheapest seats, about 1/- and found they were upstairs not in front. The programme was rather short, two small films and the big one, but the screen and talking were well up to English standards. The talk was English, a French translation was on the bottom of the picture, and Arabic and some other language were shown on a small screen at the side."

Sunday Afternoon

The wind has dropped a bit and I can now see a lorry about 50 yds. away. Some of our tents are down. There's no "hold" in this ground.

"Last night I went to bed at 8.30 and lay thinking about home. I imagined myself sitting in the armchair in front of a big fire, listening to 'Music Hall' and looking at the "Pink" (local football paper). What a wonderful life I used to have, actually, we aren't so badly off here. At least, it's dry underfoot, the food is good, we get a cigarette issue weekly and I've got a good bed. I've got three boards on low trestles, about six inches off the ground, a mattress stuffed with straw, five blankets – and a pillow. Even five blankets folded, are not enough some nights.

I wouldn't be surprised to read that this sand has filled up the sea and we will be able to ride to Italy. On second thoughts. I might be surprised. However, the fair land of Egypt is being blown away into Musso's (*Mussolini*) sea.

Our radio has broken down. That's three dud sets we've got. The best one has four valves blown, and the others may have the same trouble – or worse. It's a case of too many cooks. One section near here have a car radio. This is just the thing out here. All it needs is a car battery no H.T. It won't get S.W. but the Cairo and Jerusalem programmes are good. Jerusalem is on 449 metres, the same as North Regional, and the English station can be heard in the background. Rome and some Balkan stations come over quite well, and there are no atmospherics, which seems strange to me. I thought DXs would come through like kisses on the bottom of a letter."

Sent from 3rd Armoured Brigade, O.F.P Section, Wednesday 26th February 1941.

"Yesterday and today were something like old times. I've got hold of a motor bike, a Gilera. It's in fairly good condition, the engine, gear box and tyres are o.k., the brakes go on but won't always come off, and the front fork spring is broken. This broken spring makes the bike want to go to the right and as most of the going is soft sand, I ride very carefully.

A few days ago we stopped for the night on the sea-shore. My lorry was only about 100 yards from the sea, and of course, the sound reminded me of home. We are only about a mile from the sea here. We were in cultivated country a short while ago and it seemed beautiful after so much desert. We were all sorry when the country changed to semi-desert. It's as flat as the pancakes we didn't have yesterday (I bet you did) and scattered with poor little dried-up bushes about a foot high, some grass in places and some mauve flowers. Add quite a few camels, goats, sheep, donkeys and horses, and a ridge of sand dunes and you have the picture here."

Sent from 3rd Armoured Brigade, O.F.P Section, 9th March 1941.

"I hope the snap won't give you a shock, it isn't much like me. The others are St Sgt Thurton, Fred and Cpl. Elmy."

Sent from 3rd Armoured Brigade, O.F.P Section Sunday, 16th March 1941.

"Out of my six storemen (privates) two worked at Woolworths. One, named Nunn, was at Lowestoft for a time. His father, a retired CID Inspector, took over the

"Elephant & Castle" when Arthur Dann died, and after that lived in Long Road. On second thoughts it may have been Arthur's father at the E & C. The other man from Woolworths works in London and his flat has been badly damaged by bombs."

Sent from 3rd Armoured Brigade, O.F.P Section, Saturday 22nd March 1941. (**his birthday**)

"This famous day is nearly over. It has been the quietest birthday I have ever had. During the week I got a letter dated Dec 16th and the Journal (local newspaper) and hoped to get another letter today, but was unlucky."

Sent from 3rd Armoured Brigade, O.F.P Section, 30th March 1941.

I'm getting quite good at sand-riding on 'Alice'. It's a lovely bike. The past week has been much the same as usual except for a run into town. I went with two lorries and a trailer on Wednesday afternoon and got back after tea the next day. My lorry had a burst tyre on the way down and that delayed us. It was too late for business that night.

I was up at six, had another wash and a shave and went along to the lorries to see how the men were getting on. They were all up, so I went after some breakfast. This was three fried eggs (again) fried bacon, bread and butter and jam, and coffee. After breakfast we got busy and we were away by twelve. We went into the town a few miles away. I had a pass admitting me there on business and we got in alright, although I had another vehicle, a motor cycle dispatch rider who had brought me a message the previous night. We couldn't get what we went there for, in fact, I didn't think we would, so we parked, and had a look around.

I was surprised to see so many people about, but most of the shops were closed and bricked-up in front. We asked an M.P. where we could get some food and he directed us to a small cafe which had a board outside saying that the owner was an ally – a Greek. We were on the road again by two o'clock, but before reaching camp had a strange experience. The lorry and trailer, a captured "oiler", stopped with fuel trouble so my lorry towed them for several miles. After we had left the road and were crossing the desert we heard the "oiler" engine running. My driver stopped to take off the tow-rope and then found that he couldn't start, through slight ignition trouble. So the "oiler" towed us. After another few miles, my driver put his engine in gear and let in the clutch, and our engine started. We both came into camp under our own power, and the ignition was soon put right the next morning. I had a most enjoyable trip the first time I have ever had a real journey away from any camp and I slept on a spring bed.

A day or two ago a caravan passed here. One camel looked as if it had come from Hollywood. A veiled woman was riding and a big brass chest was hung on the side.

I had my most unpleasant duty as an NCO yesterday. I found I had to put my own L/C on a "charge", and he was found guilty and lost his stripe. I worried about the case all day but I realise now I did the right thing, although it went against the grain.

The "Lowestoft Journal", also arrived. I see that the Surveyor is going to plant trees and shrubs for use after the war.

I saw the new moon, over my left shoulder last night, March 29th at about seven o'clock. When I saw the last one I wrote that events might move fast before the next new moon. They haven't in some ways, but in East Africa we are chasing the Italians, another nice slice of their navy has been wiped out and the news of the "turn-over" in Yugoslavia is the best for a long time. I hope this moon brings happenings as good."

North Africa, Cyril back right. Others unknown.

CAPTURE

A larger version of this map can be found on page 14

BACKGROUND

The 3rd Armoured Brigade. Location: Cyrenaica. (a province of Italian Libya)

Commanded by Brigadier Reginald Gordon Ward Rimington in North Africa 1940-1941.[5]

On 22nd February 1941, Churchill decided to send British troops to Greece. Most of those forces were withdrawn from Cyrenaica. Rommel drove the British out of El Agheila. A week later he seized Mersa Brega with the aim of clearing the British out of Cyrenaica which he did by April 7th capturing two British Generals Neame, and Sir Richard O'Connor. A few weeks earlier Hitler had decided to reinforce the Italians in North Africa with

---

[5] Source: www.tankmuseum.Org 29.12.15.

German forces. Two German divisions and two additional Italian divisions were sent to Libya.

Cyril was captured in Derna, Libya on 6th April 1941. Derna is a port and was a complete change from the desert. On 30th January 1941 it was captured by the Australians from the Italians then the Germans retook it on the 6th April 1941.

The following is a transcription of an excerpt from the 3rd Armoured Brigade, Ordnance Field Park, War Diary, for April 1941, and is an appendix to a report concerning movements of 3rd A.B. O.F.P....

> "Eyewitness Report Concerning Movements of the Light Repair Section, 3A.B. and Capture of L.R.S., 5RTR, L.A.D. and part of O.F.P.
>
> Thursday 3/April/41, 0700 hrs. approx., received movement orders 0800 hrs. Departed camp at sand dunes approx. 28 km south from Magrum, and proceeded during 3/4/41 and 4/4/41 and part of 5/5/41 via BEDA FOMM water point; direct to SCELEIDIMA, EL ABIAR; BARCE; and MARAWA. Between Beda Fomm and Sceleidima two vehicles were destroyed by enemy aircraft. Near Marawa at approx. 2200 hrs. On Sat 5/4/41 we were joined by a sec. of the Ord Fd. Park, and also the L.A.D apparently complete from the 5th Battalion Tanks. Here we received "B" Ech. orders to proceed to EL MACHILI.
>
> The convoy proceeded via DERNA (reached approx., 0700 hrs. 6/4/41); and leaguered approx.

Midday 6/4/41 on the Machili – Derna track but off the main road, at approx. (S) P.3650. Convoy moved off approx. 1400 hrs. along the track towards El Machili. I was travelling in a 15 cwt seravia truck near the tail of the convoy.

Some 15 miles along the track one of our vehicles fell out with a breakdown; I stopped my truck to carry out the repairs, while the remainder except Lt. Parker and his vehicle, proceeded toward El Machili. Here we were caught up by a 15 cwt truck with Cpl. Clark from Bde. HQ. Sqn. in charge. Having carried out the repair we then proceeded along the track with these 4 vehicles, to catch up the main convoy. Lt Parker was leading these 4 vehicles, followed by the other two and myself in the rear. After travelling about another 5 miles, between 1800 and 1830 hrs. I hear M/G fire and thinking it to be aircraft I ran from my vehicle and lay down in the scrubs. The firing continued and then the vehicle which was travelling second to Lt. Parker came back along the track at top speed followed by a German car which was firing at it with a M/G mounted in the centre of the car. About six cars passed and the next one stopped at my 15 cwt and a German officer questioned my driver fitter in good English as to who they were, where they were going, where they came from, where were their comrades, if they could drive, and his last order was to turn the vehicle about and follow him, which they did. Then they proceeded along the track towards DERNA AERODROME. Some 15 mins. afterwards a few more German patrol cars came past towards Derna, and then our entire convoy came along escorted by these cars. All our vehicles were driven by our own drivers. In all there were about 15 German vehicles, and of them six were towing a gun similar to our 2 pds R.tk. gun.

Under cover of darkness I walked some 20 miles back to the track which is a bypass of Derna, and was picked up by a lorry, and I reported what had happened to an Australian Inf. Req., and was subsequently picked up by 2/Lt Etherington with a detail of 3A.B. O.F.P."[6]

"In January 1941, the British force named "Western Desert Force under command of General Richard O'Connor… executed a daring outflanking movement and took Mechili from Italian forces on 27 January.

On 7th April 1941, the Italian Armoured Division Ariete captured the British garrison at Mechili as part of Rommel's first offensive through Cyrenaica…"[7]

"On the 8th April 1941, during the withdrawal from western Cyrenaica, the commanding officer of the 3rd Armoured Brigade, Brigadier Reginald Gordon Ward Rimington, was also captured and died from his wounds shortly afterwards." [8]

---

[6] Although the above report says Machili it probably should read Mechili.

[7] Source: Wikipedia.org 21.1.16.

[8] Source: www.tankmuseum.org 29.12.15.

The front cover of the war diary of the 3rd Armoured Brigade Ordnance Field Park

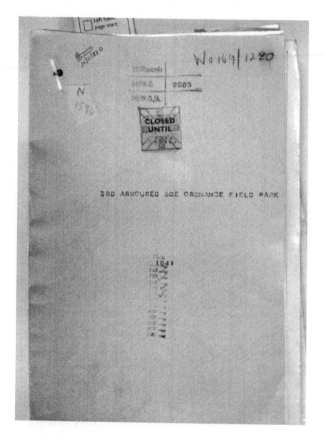

This file was originally closed until 2042. That was cancelled and the file is now open to the public and shown with the permission of The National Archives.

The 3rd Armoured Brigade Ordnance Field Park Personnel Casualty Return.

Cyril's name is shown on the fifth line down, missing believed captured.

Shown with the permission of The National Archives.

CONDITIONS AFTER CAPTURE

Large transit camps were created along the coast at Derna and Benghazi. Those captured in Libya were transported by foot and truck. Officers arriving at the transit camps were appalled at the condition of the men.

> "Those captured in the North Africa Campaign in such areas as Derna and Tobruk were frequently detained in circles of barbed wire in the middle of the desert, taken to Derna where they were left to sleep exposed in the desert, under the watch of patrolling Italian guards".[9]

> "Axis forces sought to evacuate captured personnel from forward areas as soon as possible, to reduce the logistical problems in guarding and supplying such vast numbers of demoralised prisoners and to conform to the Geneva Convention. In the aftermath of battle, large transit camps were created along the coast at Derna, Benghazi, Barce, Tripoli and Tunis, or just slightly inland as at Tarhuna. There was a great deal of improvisation, with tents often used to shelter the prisoners. At Derna, conditions were said to be primitive and chaotic. The staple diet was hard biscuit and tinned meat and even those were in short supply."[10]

---

[9] Source: 'Prisoner of War and Fugitive', (Aldershot 1947) G. H. Harris.

[10] Source: 'British Prisoners of war in Italy: Paths to Freedom', Malcolm Tudor, page 13.

"From Benghazi most sailings were across the Mediterranean to Brindisi or sometimes Taranto, on occasion via Piraeus in Greece.

The prisoners were usually confined to the crowded holds of the Italian ships. The names of these vessels are seldom mentioned in their accounts, only the dire conditions and the ever present fear that they would fall victim to attack by their own side…The only food was a little ship's biscuit, moistened with water from an occasional bucket of water that was lowered down…"The British submarine P212 Sahib sank an Italian merchantman, the S.S. Scillin, eight and a half miles off the Tunisian coast in November 1942. Sadly she was carrying over eight hundred British POWs, of whom all but twenty seven were lost."[11]

The first communication since Cyril was captured was sent to his wife, Kathleen, from 2/Lt F B Etherington reporting that Cyril was missing and was dated May 1941

In it he says:

"I had to report the news myself, and though my informant did not actually recognize your husband I think there is no doubt that he was taken prisoner.

---

[11] Source 'British Prisoners of war in Italy: Paths to Freedom', by Malcolm Tudor, page 14/15.

My informant tells me that the German officer in charge had warned his guards to treat the English prisoners well, in fact had threatened an extreme penalty if they so much as stole a button off them". I mention this because there is sometimes talk about prisoners not being treated well.

I liked Cyril, I found his quiet sense of humour delightful; and also, being an inexperienced officer, I found his experience and reliability invaluable."

This communication was followed by Army Form B. 104 - 83 from the R.A.O.C record office in Leicester stating that Cyril was posted as "missing".

A Memorandum attached to this form set out the steps taken for tracing missing personnel and the last paragraph says;

> "It should be borne in mind that the announcements of the names of prisoners of war by German wireless stations are made for the purpose of inducing people in this country to listen to German views. The lists are incomplete and often inaccurate and should not be relied upon."

Prisoner of War Leaflet

This leaflet was published on behalf of The War
Organisation of the British Red Cross Society and the
Order of St. John, in January 1942. It was the first
authentic account of the lives of British prisoners of war
in enemy hands. It sought to inform and reassure the
relatives.

At last a letter arrived from Cyril. It was dated Sunday May 18th 1941. It contained no 'from' address. Fourteen lines were allowed.

"I am a prisoner of war in Italy and am fit and well. We are allowed parcels up to 11lbs of cigarettes, toiletries and writing materials etc. Don't forget that each day is one less towards the end of the war."

> 'The Ex-prisoners of war do not often write about the transit from battlefield to a more or less permanent camp in Italy in any great detail. One may surmise this is because it was such a harrowing experience.'[12]

Cyril was no exception. He made no mention of the hardships of this journey. In fact he conveyed a very rosy picture

Sent from Campo P.G. Capua, Campo 66, Italy, 26th May 1941.

(CAPUA (Camp 66) was a transit camp situated 16 miles north of Naples. It was made up of tents, and wooden and stone huts.)

"Now that we can put our address, I can describe the scene. In the distance I can see

---

[12] Source: 'British Prisoners of war in Italy: Paths to Freedom', by Malcolm Tudor, page 13.

Vesuvius with a thin trail of smoke rising from it. Then there is a range of mountains stretching right across as far as I can see, the camp being at the foot of the hills. Between them and me is a river which winds down past Capua about a mile away. On Saturday we were visited by a priest who gave a short address in very good English, I can't remember the actual words but I won't forget the idea. He said,

> 'We honour you as brave men who answered your country's call. Now you are prisoners as many of our own comrades are, continue to be brave; don't lose heart because you are in captivity. Remember your comrades who were killed and wounded, and thank God that you were spared. Don't waste your time here, but think about and pray for your loved ones at home and go back to them a better man'

This is advice I will try to carry out."

CAMPO 78

By June 1941 Cyril had been moved to Campo 78, Sulmona, 100 miles east of Rome and 2,000 feet up in the Apennine Mountains. It was built on the mountain slope at the edge of the village of Fonte d' Amore. The Apennine Mountains are the highest in the region. Mount Morrone, at 6,762 ft. soared up high behind Campo 78. During WW2 it contained 3,000 British and Commonwealth prisoners. During WW1 it housed Austrian POWs.

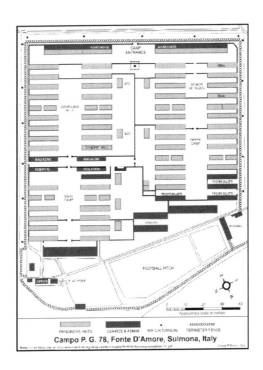

Campo P. G. 78, Fonte D'Amore, Sulmona, Italy

Sent from Campo 78, 2nd June 1941.

"As you can see by the address we have moved, this time to a permanent camp. The big event of the week was the arrival on Wednesday of parcels from the Red Cross. There was a parcel between each two men and in addition 26 "Gold Flake" each.

The parcels contained tinned food, biscuits etc. And are valued at about 10/- each. "We had twelve of our Section in our tent so we pooled tea, cocoa, Ovaltine, and sugar, Nestles and powdered milk and shared out the tinned food to each pair of men.

I had a half share in tins of baked beans, Morton's M & V Syrup, meat loaf and margarine and also some plain chocolate. It seems that every man gets a parcel a month. In this camp the men have been getting one between four each week, which is better than waiting a month. The Red Cross representatives came on the same day and inspected the camp and answered questions.

I have heard that the Red Cross will send you a label every three months. I do know that parcels and mail are post free, but an air mail letter has a 5d stamp and gets here in two weeks.

We arrived here yesterday. I was in a 2nd class carriage, only three men to a seat in a corridor coach, so we had plenty of room. We travelled at night and were able to sleep all the while it was dark, especially as the trains over here run so smoothly. I woke about five to find we were in mountainous county and being pulled by an electric engine which are used a lot here. The scenery was wonderful, cultivated valleys hemmed in by mountains, some still with snow on top. Sulmona is in a valley, as far as I can judge, about ten miles by five. I can see the railway running along a mountain side in the distance. The camp is built against a cliff and we can see right across the valley which is flat We had about a three mile walk from the station along a winding lane, over small streams and under trees, with wild roses and honeysuckle in the hedges. When we arrived the Sergeants were sent to a separate compound. I am in a long room with about 25 beds on each side. Buff is also here, and Percy Parker and some others. They are in another part, and I haven't seen them yet.

We are given 2 loaves in the morning and two hot meals, at about 11.30 and 5.30. We hand one loaf back to the cookhouse for serving at meals and use the other for breakfast."

"…the ration bread would be cut with utmost care. Some prisoners used the width of the metal POW tag as a guide to thickness, others would observe the act of cutting with fanatical attention to detail, such was the importance of the act. ….The bread ration would also be a test of the personal traits of the individual. And two main types appeared: hoarders and bashers. Hoarders would save at least part of their bread ration to have as breakfast: Bashers would eat theirs there and then and go hungry later."[13]

Obviously, Cyril and his companions fell into a well-known pattern and were what was known as 'hoarders'.

RED CROSS PARCELS

In WW2 Red Cross parcels were arranged in accordance with the Geneva Convention of 1929. Every POW was supposed to be sent a 5kg parcel four times a month but

---

[13] Source: 'Prisoner of War In Germany', page 17 by Peter Doyle, Shire Publications Ltd, 2011.

delivery was often disrupted. Several receipts for Red Cross parcels received by Cyril have survived, all were from the Canadian Red Cross.

Contents of Canadian Red Cross Parcels

Sixteen ounces of milk powder
Eight ounces of sugar
Sixteen ounces of butter
Sixteen ounces of jam or honey
Four Ounces of cheese
Sixteen ounces of pilot biscuits
Twelve ounces of corned beef
Eight ounces of chocolate
Ten ounces of pork luncheon meat
One ounce of salt and pepper
Eight ounces of salmon (mustard, onion
powder and other condiments
Four ounces of sardines or kippers
also sometimes enclosed)
Eight ounces of dried apples
Four ounces of tea or coffee
Eight ounces of dried prunes or raisins
Two ounces of soap[14]

British Red Cross Parcels

"The Red Cross is able to buy bulk supplies on special terms and is granted duty-free prices by the Customs and Excise Department, which means that articles are much cheaper than they would be if bought in a shop….. The average cost

---

[14] Source: Wikipedia.org/wiki/red_cross_parcel 16.1.2016.

of a parcel works out as a total of £10. This does not include freight to Geneva, which is now about 1s 2d per parcel, but which will shortly be reduced, it is hoped, to about 9d."[15]

Sent from Campo 78, Saturday 14th June 1941

"A handball league has been started in this compound. A man (not a player) stands at each end of the pitch with his arms up stretched. To score, the ball must pass between his arms. When the ball bounces off his face it's too bad. There's rather a shortage of volunteers for this job.

The garden was planted by the men who were here when we came, and they put in potatoes etc. A small spring runs near and the water is led through channels to irrigate the garden.

When I peeled potatoes, eight of us were all morning and half the afternoon on the job.

I'm thinner than when you last saw me and I expect to get thinner still when the hot weather arrives. I have a walk each evening round and round the compound. I spend quite a lot of time reading, a Penguin book lasting me about a day and a half. When I've

[15] Source: The Prisoner of War Journal, June 1943 page 15.

**read all the books here I may send you a list
of books I would like, Smiths are the only
people who can send books to us."**

Sport was encouraged as it was believed that it relieved
aggression. Also, it could be removed as a punishment.

The Royal Horticultural Society began sending seeds to
prison camps in 1941 through the Red Cross. Gardening
became a favourite pastime and often brought good
results.

A letter from the Regimental Paymaster in Leeds, to
Cyril's wife, arrived dated 17th June 1941, confirming
continuation of payment of family allowance to her.

> "....while expressing deep sympathy we feel that
> you will wish to know that the family allowance at
> present being paid to you on his behalf will be
> continued until 5.10.41 at 35/6 per week."

Sent from Campo 78, Saturday 28th June 1941.

**"Another week has gone by, one less to wait
for mail. The hot weather has made the older
inhabitants talk about last winter and how
cold it was. We seem to be well up in the
mountains, but I don't expect it to be as cold
as England. I was wearing battle dress and a
brand new pair of boots when I was captured
and I've got my overcoat so the cold won't
trouble me.**

Can you order me the following books through Smiths (post free)

Corduroy	Penguin no. 247
Twenty-Five	Penguin no. 7
Away from it all	Penguin no. 254[16]

Looking out over the valley I can see that the scene has changed in the four weeks I have been here, Instead of a green valley, I see fields of ripening corn in various shades of gold. The snow is nearly gone from the mountains and the mountains themselves are dimmed during the day by a heat-haze.

Far up the valley to the north-west where the sun has set, is a blue mountain and behind that mountain is you. So near but great barriers between."

Sent from Campo 78 (Compound 2), Monday 14th July 1941.

---

[16]The Penguin Book Co. ran a service of new Penguin books to prisoners of war. Also, camp libraries were set up by Camp Leaders and were supplied by the Indoor Recreations Section of the Prisoners of War Department. Requests were received for books about English country life and plays for the prisoners to perform.

Another week nearer that mail.

"I see that Yarmouth has been bombed several times lately. Buck up Lowestoft."

It seems as if news of home was getting through not only from letters from family but via secret radio sets.

Sent from Campo 78. (Compound 2), Monday 21st July 1941

"It was my turn this morning to go out for a walk. We left at nine o'clock and were out for about two hours, so we did five or six miles. Soon after leaving camp we passed through a small village and then went down a county road until we came to a main road. Here we turned and came back the same way. Although the roads are lined with hedges and trees, it is not an English scene. The trees are tall and upright, not spreading, and the land is not divided into fields.

On the way back I could see our camp at the foot of the cliff. Above this cliff the hillside goes up as high again, is covered with trees which look like pines. I am told they were planted by prisoners during the last war.

And so another week passes, still with hopes that our mail will come soon."

Sent from Campo 78. (Compound 2), 28th July 1941.

"Your birthday, Many Happy Returns. It is certain that those to come will be happier than this. On Monday I had a game of Basket Ball. We have proper goals now, with baskets. One of these days I shall have plenty of mail."

Sent from Campo 78 (Compound 2), 5th August 1941.

"Friday was the Great Day; your first letter arrived. The postman passed me at first and then came back with one letter calling "Evans". I hope he'll soon get to know my name very well. Your letter took only 21 days to get here. There is so much news in your letter that I can't answer it in 24 lines.

Last Monday we were visited by the Papal Nuncio[17], who brought a personal message of blessing and good wishes from the Pope. We

[17]POPE PIUS X11. In 1941 Pope Pius X11 appointed a Papal Nuncio to minister to the spiritual and material needs of the prisoners.

each got one of the enclosed cards as a memento of the visit.

Our walks now start at 7.30am and we are back before it gets too hot. Saturday must be market day in Sulmona as we saw women going there carrying baskets on their heads. Most of them wore brightly coloured blouses and I suppose they had eggs etc.

We have a commercial artist here and he and his assistants have produced a newspaper the "Compound Courier". There is only one copy and it hasn't come to me yet." The election campaign is going strong to elect the Mayor of Compound City. More later."

Sent from Campo 78 (Compound 2), 12th August 1941

"I haven't received your second letter up to today, Sunday, although I've watched the postman carefully each night lately. I have been reading a good book. "Ragged Banners". Part is about Italy, then the girl goes to her cottage in Suffolk with "that salt smell of the sea, earthy scent of bracken and bitter-sweet of sun-warmed gorse" The cottage is between Walberswick and Aldeburgh."

Sent from Campo 78 (Compound 2,) Sunday 19th August 1941.

"I had another letter from you early in the week but the snap had been removed by the censor. I was disappointed, but I realize objects in the background of snaps could convey a message. I hear that studio photos in separate envelopes are allowed but don't know if this is official. Not having the picture I can't guess where you spent your holiday, so you'll have to tell me. I feel very bucked to receive such happy letters – keep it up.

The past week has been very full. In addition to Pass-ball, we have had several heats of our sports, the finals being on Aug. 31st. In the evenings we have had several Jumble Bees (films, spelling, tunes, charades etc.) We had a mock trial the other evening. The trial was a libel action by the RAF against the 'Compound Courier' for saying "It seems by the number of airmen here that the RAF can't find Malta." After the first few minutes the trial became serious and was very interesting. The judge (a barrister's clerk) and the two counsel were very good and the questioning and cross-examination of witnesses was clever. The case was adjourned - so more later.

I have written to the **Paymaster** asking him to send you £20. Did you get the £2 and £5 I sent before I was captured?"[18]

Army Form O 1690 confirming an extra payment

[The printing on reverse is cancelled.]

Army Form O 1690.

~~The Cashier,~~

Regimental .... ~~Command,~~

Pay master Leeds.

forwards herewith a { ~~Money Order~~ / ~~Postal Order~~ / Postal Draft } for

£20 —————

being the amount ~~due to you for~~ of a remittance authorized by your husband.

Date 1. 10. 41 19

(18448) Wt.3274/945 500,000 11/40 A.& E,W.Ltd. Gp.698
Forms/O 1690/25.

---

[18] Ironically even though he was a POW Cyril's permission had to be gained before the Paymaster could make extra payments to his wife.

Sent from Campo 78. (Compound 2), 26th August 1941.

"Our 'Compound Courier', says that two Bette Davis Films are very good, "All This and Heaven Too" and "The Letter." I have been playing a lot of chess lately, mainly with a man who was in Lowestoft a few years ago. He knows the "Norfolk Hotel" and "Godetia". There is a suggestion that we should have a one-act play but the trouble is getting someone to write it. There would be five in a team, hero, heroine, villain, father and an effects man. The only costume would be a moustache for the villain."

Sent from Campo 78 (Compound 2), Friday 29th August 1941.

"I am very glad to hear you are spending a lot of time in the garden. Things must be quieter this year up above. (*A reference to bombing.*) Have you seen the 2$^{1/2d}$ letter cards for prisoners of war? I walked to the door and saw the new moon at about seven.

Sent from Campo 78 (Compound 2), 2nd September 1941

"Today is our sports day. The Pass-ball league finished on Friday with the Angels good winners with 33 points out of 34. Our

Lord Mayor presented trophies to the teams. He was dressed in top hat and a frock coat, a lovely chain of office (mainly silver paper and tin) and a monocle. The league trophy is a model of a goal post with net and ball, standing on a round block. On the block are places for names of winners. The five angels and a reserve each received a plaque, an oval about one and a half by one inch. These plaques were carved from pieces of red tile, with borders, lettering and shield in relief, and are works of art.

I have been getting a **Red Cross Parcel** each week lately and I hear this will continue. You say you are allowed only one sheet of notepaper. Is this official? I saw a letter with four single-sided sheets of air mail paper. If you are only allowed one, those letter cards will be best at two for 5^d."

Sent from Campo 78 (Compound 2), 9th September 1941.

"It is a fortnight tomorrow since my last letter. My four is now a long way behind **Les Turton's 30**. Fred is also out of luck. He has heard this week from his daughter, niece and neighbour but not from his wife. The censor has passed on the snap and I think you spent your holiday on the farm near **Bungay**. I can't see any change in you in a year but you aren't smiling so I think I like the one of us at the wedding best.

We finished our sports on Tuesday and that evening the Mayor presented the prizes. The winner of each event received a coloured card by Briggs[19] our artist showing three boys in the uniforms of the services running arm in arm with a ball and chain dragging along behind. First second and third in each event received 25, 15 and 10 cigarettes (1,400 were contributed). A trophy was given to the room scoring most points. This was a circle about 9 inches across cut from a tree and with Royal coat of arms, Room trophy etc. drawn. On the face in colours. The relay winners got a wooden shield hand carved with a relay runner and lettering. Both these trophies are very good indeed, especially as the carving was probably by razor blade."

---

[19] "Robert Roden Briggs was a Commercial Artist and Cartoonist. His cartoon diary was published after his death into a book entitled 'A funny Kind of War'…he used to bribe the guards with anything and everything he could to get him pencils, paper and paint." Source Moosburg.org Stalag V11A: Oral history, 27.1.16.

Sent from Campo 78 (Compound 2), 16th September 1941.

"My mail has arrived today, Sunday – your letter of Aug 6th and well worth waiting for.

Fred had letters from his daughter, niece and neighbour. Now he has got the first from his wife, with the terrible news that his only boy had been killed testing a motorcycle at the Depot. Of course, he was very upset and when I saw him I said nothing about it, however, he came in yesterday and we had a cup of tea and a smoke. We were telling the two 'haggises' about the good times in France and in England. Fred mentioned the trouble he had to get twelve hours leave on a Saturday night when his boy was home on leave- the last time he saw him. That was all that was said about it."

Sent from Campo 78 (Compound 2), 23rd September 1941.

"We have formed an orchestra, the instruments are made of cardboard, silver paper. Etc. On the 'paper and comb' principle. A concert is on this weekend. Sat Sunday and Monday – two rooms a night. We go on Monday.

We had a good dinner today, Morton's Steak and Kidney Pudding and with biscuits, some cheese from Waveney Drive, bread and blackberry jelly and tea.

I wonder if you will be able to get some blackberries this year. I've a feeling I'll be seeing them next year, and that's the general feeling here. Those who don't think next autumn, think next spring. So it's up to England to prove who are right."

The fact that music was a tremendous comfort to the POWs was recognized by the International Red Cross and the Indoor Recreations Section dispatched musical instruments. Instruments provided by the Red Cross had not reached Cyril and his companions at this time. In 1944 The Prisoner of War journal noted that:-

> "…In the early months of 1941, ten complete orchestras consisting of fourteen instruments were dispatched to the larger camps in Germany. ….Gifts of second-hand music began to pour in to the Indoor Recreations Section as the result of next of kin receiving constant requests from prisoners for music of all kinds… In addition the Section began to purchase music on a large scale.
>
> The service to individual prisoners of forwarding instruments either belonging to the prisoner or procured on behalf of the next of kin had been begun early in 1941… During 1942 and 1943 the

chief work of the Indoor Recreations Section was to supply camps in Italy. This was not achieved without difficulty. In fact, it was only just before the transfer of British prisoners to Germany in the summer of 1943 that adequate supplies of books, indoor games and musical instruments were reaching Italy."[20]

---

[20] Source: 'Prisoner of War' Journal September 1944 page 13.

The. 'Prisoner of War' Journal

This journal was sent free to the next of kin who registered with the Prisoners of War Department. Because of the paper shortage at the time no copies were for sale.

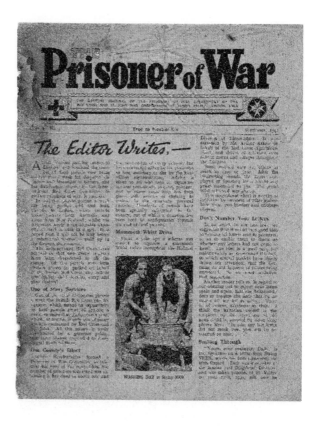

Sent from Campo 78. (Compound 2), 1ˢᵗ October 1941.

"Fred's wife has had an Income Tax demand for £24 for the year to be paid £2 a month. So be prepared.

A few parcels have come in, and this week we are having a half-issue of a New Zealand parcel.

I went for a walk on Monday morning; I had an old pair of trousers given me. The walk, or march, was very enjoyable. Rain on Sunday evening had laid the dust, and there was a nip in the air. We went on our usual route and were out for 1 and a half hours.

We played cricket against Fred's compound on Sunday afternoon and I was one of the lucky ones to go through. All the boys are OK. We lost the match 35 and 6 against 5 their 24 and 20 not out, using proper bats and wickets and a tennis ball. The pitch has been made by smoothing the top part of their roadway, and all bowling is uphill. Quite a steep slope. I don't think a cyclist could ride up. Catches after the ball had hit a roof or wall were O.K., so a batsman would swipe a ball over the bungalows and then a cheer from the spectators in line with the openings would tell him he was out."

In 1942 The Prisoner of War journal noted this under the title Uphill Cricket.

> "Sport at P.G. 78 (Sulmona) is very popular, but the cricket is not very MCC. Apparently the pitch has a gradient of one in four, (there is one wicket at the top of the hill) and "You can be caught out off a roof or wall of the huts around."[21]

Sent from Campo 78. (Compound 2), 7th October 1941.

"I was wondering if you had my letter about books – now I see they are on the way. Thank you. My name was on the parcels list the other day but after waiting in the queue there was nothing for me – only a clerical error. Still, patience is my strong point and it's getting stronger.

It is now six months since I was captured, but it doesn't seem that long. Although each day is full there are no landmarks to mark the passing of months."

---

[21] Source: 'The Prisoner of War' journal, Sept. 1942 page 7.

Sent from Campo 78. (Compound 2), 10th October 1941.

"So my photo has been in the paper, did it say under 'caught unarmed'?"

The paper mentioned was the' Lowestoft Journal' and it appeared in the 6th September 1941 edition. [22]

Sgt. Cyril Henry Evans, husband of Mrs. K. A. Evans, Kathrill Walmer Road, Lowestoft, who is a prisoner of war in Italy.

---

[22] Source: The Heritage Centre, Lowestoft.

Sent from Campo 78. (Compound 2), 14th October 1941.

"The YMCA is sending Educational Courses and while waiting for the text books to come, we are starting classes in maths, French, Italian and German. (also Elementary Bookkeeping)

The Courier published the Income/tax rates and I got a shock. It seems that after the war I shall pay nearly £50 a year.

"I went for a walk yesterday. The leaves are falling and the grape harvest is being gathered. I saw several parties of women in brightly coloured dresses, in the fields. As we passed one of the carts loaded with tubs of grapes, the driver gave me a big bunch. Fred Dugan was with me."

Sent from Campo 78 (Compound 2), 21st October 1941.

"We had the first snow on the hills on Monday October 13. Since then the weather has been warm again and the only snow in sight is on the highest mountains.

I'm glad Mr. Etherington wrote to you. I last saw him in the middle of a certain night and

then lost him again. If I could have kept with him I would have got away.

A general Middle East clothing parcel came the other day and I drew a pyjama suit, so I'm alright for clothing, except socks. Chocolate is very nice, unless it's about 10/- a slab when I wouldn't like it so much.

Our padre is arranging a Christmas gift to the Red Cross. He would like us to ask our people to send in a certain sum, and then he will tell the Red Cross that a gift of 'so much' has been made by the prisoners at Sulmona. Can we afford £1?"[23]

Sent from Campo 78. (Compound 2), 28th October 1941.

"No more mail so far except your telegram on the 21st and six books on the 24th. A lot were handed out last night so perhaps my turn will come tonight.

Uncle Lush who used to sleep beside me has taken charge of the cookhouse in another

---

[23] Perhaps the thinking behind a collection for the Red Cross from prisoners receiving Red Cross parcels was that there were prisoners in other areas who were worse off.

compound. In the early part of the war the new man was near Darsham for three months, so he knows Lowestoft, Ipswich, Southwold, Dunwich, Leiston etc.

Do you go to the cinema now? I hear that 'Come live with me' and 'Married but single' are good."

Sent from Campo 78. (Compound 2), 4th November 1941.

"The photo is lovely darling I have covered it in cellophane and made a cardboard frame. It is hanging on the wall beside my shelf of books."

Sent from Campo 78 (Compound 2), 7th November 1941.

"I should like a Hugo's French- English Pocket Dictionary @ 2/6, also Hugo's French Reading Simplified @ 3/6. I think Smith's will be able to send them for you[24] I have won a string mat in a draw and it's very handy at the side of my bed – better than concrete. I suppose you'll have some of the slip mats finished by the time you get this. It won't be long before I am standing on them.

---

[24] She did send the books and he did receive them.

About the only thing I am likely to want are socks, so if you send two pairs in every parcel it will be OK. Don't spend too much on chocolate, I'll only eat it. About a pound each three months will be plenty."

The amount of chocolate allowed in next-of-kin parcels was restricted and later increased as reported below.

> "By arrangement with the Ministry Food, the quantity of solid slab chocolate which may be purchased from the Packing Centre…for inclusion in Next-of-Kin quarterly parcels sent to Prisoners of War will be increased from 1lb to $1^{1/2}$lb. …The price per pound will remain the same, and the Red Cross will continue to supply an additional half pound of gift chocolate if weight allows. Next of kin may also add any quantity of solid slab chocolate which they have obtained with their own sweet ration coupons."[25]

Sent from Campo 78. (Compound 2), 11th November 1941.

"The snow on the hills looks as if it's there until spring. This time next year I shall be enjoying November fogs.

---

[25] Source: The Prisoner of War journal September 1942 page 14.

I went for a walk the other day and saw Buff, Percy Parker and Bill Challis. I wasn't able to speak to them but they look well. I haven't seen Jerry King (Ipswich) since we came here, but Bill Chaplin is now in this compound.

I hear that women of 29 have registered. I suppose I'll soon hear you are called-up. England now realises there's a war on and all that it means. Every extra woman at work means one more man fighting.

If you are still on 1 hour summer time we are an hour ahead of you. So at 11 on Christmas and New Year's Eve I shall be thinking of you."

Sent from Campo 78. (Compound 2), 18th November 1941.

"The rain stops us walking around the pitch, but when it gets colder and freezes, we will be warmer. I am wearing my overcoat as I write. A year ago today, Saturday, I was sweating in the tropics while natives sold us bananas and oranges. Now I am at the other extreme – a prisoner- but next year the pendulum will have swung back and I shall be home.

Fred Dugan had his 46th birthday on the 13th."

Sent from Campo 78. (Compound 2), 25th November 1941.

"This war has taught me things too – to take no notice of disappointments, to eat dry bread, and like it, when our parcel is finished, and to always look forward to better times. I saw the new moon after tea on Thursday the 20th and I wondered if you were looking at it too."

Sent from Campo 78 (Compound 2), 2nd December 1941.

"I went to the store on Saturday for food parcels and saw Buff and Fred. I've just read "Our Bill" by Freddy Grisewood.

We are being paid 10 lire a week and this month I have ordered honey, milk tobacco and matches. I don't know if this comes out of our pay."

Sent from Campo 78. (Compound 2), 9th December 1941.

"I heard from Uncle Joe this week but that's all the mail I've had. We have been visited by representatives of the Red Cross from Geneva. They spent some time in this compound talking with the Italian officers and our representative, and took two snaps, neither with me on but one with my two Scots pals at an open air maths class. They said they would try to send us blackboards and chalk. I think I told you we were being paid 10 lire a week. Well, the first part of our order has come in, and I have got my tobacco and matches. Part of the condensed milk came and I was lucky enough to draw a tin."

Sent from Campo 78. (Compound 2), 16th December 1941.

"I heard Bob Hunter has died. He transferred to the Indian Army and took his wife and boy out there. Another friend of mine Quartermaster Sergeant Smith, has been killed at Tobruk. Time for something more cheerful now. We have a piano in the mess, and last week's concert was even better than usual.

I hear that our Woolworths has been hit. Is that right? The newspaper says that we are going to call up men of 18 up to 51. In spite of

the spread of the war, most of us here think we shall be home for next Christmas."[26]

A resident of Lowestoft, A. J. Turner, sent letters to his son during WW2. Some of these have been published online by G. A. Michael Sims. Below is an entry.

'Letters from Lowestoft' - A J Turner

"Monday 5th May 1941 – The heavier bombs were placed on London Road again. I went to see in the morning. Woolworth's was bombed and burned and is completely destroyed. There are several 'Delayed Action' bombs about and they have been going off all day- now 5.40pm"[27]

---

[26] Lowestoft. "In World War Two, the town was heavily targeted for bombing by the Luftwaffe due to its engineering industry and role as a naval base. It is sometimes claimed that it became one of the most heavily bombed towns per head of population in the UK." 13th January 1942 was the worst day of bombing during WW2 for Lowestoft."
Source en.m.wikipedia.org 29.1.16.

[27] Source: www.oldlowestoft.co.uk

Sent from Campo 78. (Compound 2), 26th December 1941.

"We were visited the other day by the Papal Nuncio.[28] He brought us Christmas Greetings from the Pope and gave us a card each. This is on the card – "With ever-greater paternal solicitude we turn our thoughts to each of you who, in your separation from distant homes at this Christmas Season, feel very keenly the absence of your loved ones. May our prayerful and affectionate good wishes sweeten the bitterness of that separation and be to you all a source of divine comfort and Christian hope."

This is a lovely day – not a cloud in the sky – and the mountains snow-covered. It is quite warm out here this afternoon and the air is always lovely. Still, it would be better by the fire with the nutcrackers busy, the radio on and rain outside."

---

[28] Emissaries from the Pope visited the camps at Christmastime in 1942 and gave each prisoner a Christmas carol and calendar.

Sent from Campo 78. (Compound 2), 30th December 1941.

"I hope you have had a good Christmas. Our cooks had saved the meat ration for a few days and our officers sent us some more cigarettes (80 Italian each) cake and cheese. Our combine had saved a tin of bacon and butter. As it was too cold to go to the whist drive we went to bed at 8. I am writing this in bed, with a blizzard outside."

From Campo 78 – Sulmona.

The Christmas card below was sent from Campo 78 and had been signed by Briggs the commercial artist and cartoonist.

Sent from Campo 78. (Compound 2), 20TH January 1942.

"**The sun is shining today, Sunday, after a wet week. There is too much mud to walk about at present. I am taking care of myself, and the winter is nearly over. I now have a third blanket and a new pair of boots, so I'm OK for the rest of the winter.**"

Sent from Campo 78. (Compound 2), 27th January 1942.

"**I have been walking with two men in the London catering business, one a Lyons inspector and the other at the Regent Palace Hotel. The subject has been food and I've collected ideas on where to live and what to eat in London. Bed breakfast and bath is about 9/- at the Regent (16/6 double). The breakfast is big enough to last till the evening meal.**

I had a new battle dress issue yesterday and it's warmer than the old one, which had worn very thin. Our cooks often put the cabbage through the mincer and make a very nice thick soup on meatless days."

A letter from the R.A.O.C. Record Office, Edward Wood Hall, London Road, Leicester, dated 28th January 1942, was sent to Cyril's wife informing her of a message having been broadcast for her by Vatican City Radio, on 13.1.1942, from British Prisoners of War in Italy and picked up in this country."[29]

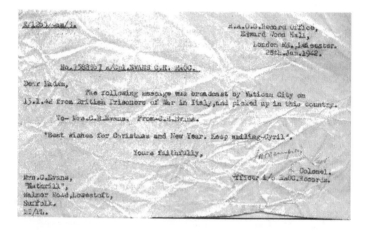

Sent from Campo 78. (Compound 2), 3rd February 1942.

"I had a woolen scarf given me before Christmas and I stitched it up the back and wear it as a hat. Bob has given me a RAF shirt and I have made a tie. So I look smart today. I'll use them on Sundays only. I gave my new boots a good dose of C.W.C. polish

---

[29] Vatican City pursued a policy of neutrality during World War 11, under the leadership of Pope Pius X11.

from that tin we bought before the war. It's still good. Good old Co-op."

Sent from Campo 78. (Compound 2), 17th February 1942.

"Today Sunday we woke up to see the deepest snow yet. We hoped the worst of the winter was over.

Our normal rations are macaroni for lunch, and a plate of stew and a plate of rice at five. We also get about 1lb bread a day. Simple, but enough especially for this easy life. We also get an issue of fat (fried bread once a week) wine, etc. I saw all our lads last Sunday and they are well and in good spirits. Fred, Buff, and Percy Parker send their regards. I hadn't seen some of them since June 1st and the change is surprising. At a whist drive a dozen eggs were auctioned. They fetched £3 were put back again and made another £2, then Jock's father bought them for £1.

A nice lady in America has adopted 50 soldiers (40 officers and 10 men) to send food and clothing to."

Sent From Camp 78. (Compound 2), 3rd March 1942.

"The weather has improved a lot. The snow line is well up the hills now. I've got through the winter very well, no bad colds and no chilblains. Some chaps have had sore fingers for some time."

Sent from Campo 78. (Compound 2), 10th March 1942.

"I had my 27th letter from you last night (dated Feb 13th) that's 61 letters, cards and parcels since Aug 2nd – 31 weeks."

Spring is here. Six of us have got together. We crawl out about 8o/c and stretch and bend – very gently. We are all stiff; through spending most of winter in bed. After a day or two will do a little running. Senior ranks are now in a separate compound so I don't see Fred. We get a much better view of the valley as we are right up the slope. I've been reading Beverley Nichols' "Village in the Valley".

Bob Haxton had his 25th birthday. We (our combine) each gave half a loaf to make a cake. The bread was grated into crumbs and mixed with raisins, prunes, tangerine peel and water. We cooked it under the galley stove, put **Happy Returns** on top in thick milk and had it for supper. I'm having one on the 22nd."

Sent from Campo 78. (Compound 2), 17th March 1942.

"I see in today's paper that petrol will no longer be used for private purposes in England. About time too! You should hear some chaps when they get a letter saying that some relation in the army in England has only one day off a week and is at least 20 miles from a town, instead of having a nice long holiday in a prison camp. Still, it doesn't affect me like that; I still listen for the bagpipes over the hills."

Sent from Compo 78 (Compound 2), 24th March 1942. (written on 22nd)

"This is my birthday. It was a lovely evening, but as usual it had a sad feeling. Perhaps it's because it's the end of a wasted day that is gone forever. However, fine mornings make me very happy. The sun first shines on the peak at the end of the valley, behind which is you and home. Then it shines on the mountain opposite. The snow on both has a pink glow against a pale clear blue sky and the hills in front are a deep blue-grey. As the sun rises behind me the snow turns white, the hills turn blue, brown and green, and the flat valley stands out clearly. There are thousands of fruit trees in blossom, like dandelion clocks, and many white houses, many more than can be seen in the summer when the trees are in leaf."

Sent from Campo 78. (Compound 2), 31st March 1942.

"Another Sunday – Palm Sunday. Last year, on Palm Sunday (April 6th) at about this time 2.30pm, I was captured.

This is a diary of my birthday.

Woke about 7.30 Daydreamed until 8.30 no PT on Sunday
Many 'Happy Returns' from all, for Clarence Copeland and me, he was 29.
9.00 Tea water. A cup of tea with milk and 1/3 loaf saved from yesterday spread with jam. Then sit outside reading.
11.00 Muster (when we line up to be counted)
11.30 A new lodger arrives.
12.00 "Come and Get It" clear soup.
12.45 Tea water as at 9.0 but using new loaf which has just come.

1.00 Write to you – then read.

3.00 Church.

3.30 Read.

4.30 Wash.

5.00 'Come and Get It', a meat day so we have stew and minced meat, beans macaroni and turnip tops then boiled rice.

6.00 Tea water – as before – and 1/3 loaf saved for next day.

6.30 Stroll.

7.00 Make bed.

8.00 Get in.

8.30 Sleep.

The YMCA (Geneva) has sent quite a lot of books, and all sorts of classes are going strong. I fall asleep to a talk of balance sheets and wake up to algebra."

Sent from Campo 78 (Compound 2), 7th April 1942.

"On one day there were 35 parcels for every 100 men. Bob had cigarettes and books, Jock had text books (3) on optics. The food was very welcome. It was shared out and the balance was drawn for so each man had something extra. I had – 1 lb. butter, 1 lb. cheese 1 1/2 lbs. M & V, a half lb. jam, 3oz meat extract, 4ozs sugar 1 tablet carbolic

soap (all from **Argentina**) and **90** gold Flake.
I've been eating thin slices of bread, spread
with butter, extract and cheese "big eats".
The **M&V** didn't get a chance to go bad and
I've kept water on the butter.

Sent from Campo 78. (Compound 2), 7 May 1942.

"I don't think I'll send one of my cards to the
Town Hall. They don't seem to trouble over
me — very few letters, no war bonus, and no
cigarettes for Xmas and haven't been round
to see if you are managing alright.

I wonder how many more New Moons.
Surely it can't be far off now. Soon after my
capture I told you twelve I may not be far
wrong. It's up to you in England.

I was sorry to read of the heavy bombing of
Norwich and Exeter. All I can do is use all
my patience. It's nearly three weeks since I
heard from you. It seems a lifetime. I think
I've said that several times before — so I must
have spent several 'lifetimes' here. But I
might be worse off. Thank God I'm not still
in the desert, sleeping on cases, food
smothered in sand, and a ration of salty
water. One day I'll be eating fish and chips,
cream doughnuts, eggs and bacon, fried

sausages, listening to the radio, watching the flowers grow."

Sent from Campo 78. (Compound 2), 14th May 1942.

"One year since I crossed the Med; expecting to be rescued or sunk by the Navy.

Football was stopped for a time because we were 'bad boys' but started again yesterday.

The chap next to me tried to argue about herrings. Nearly all these new parcels have two 1oz tins of Morton's Bloater Paste (containing 74% herring) In spite of what I said, he told me that kippers were smoked herrings, but bloaters were a different fish, but of the same family. Of course, I let it go at that, he was so sure about it.

We are still enjoying our 'bridge' although we have only won 5 out of 16 and have minus 23,250 points.

I'm glad you heard from Fred Holder. I didn't know his unit or number when I sent the card in September. He may find out that he can write to me through Red Cross, 9 Sharia Malika Farida, Cairo. Usual time 3 months. Fred and I were good friends and we used to go about with Cyril Connell in Alexandria. A sergeant, lance corporal and a private. Strictly against the rules."

Sent from Campo 78. (Compound 2), 28th May 1942.

"We had a very enjoyable afternoon yesterday, going down to see an Art Exhibition by the Yugo-slav prisoners. There were a dozen or more portraits by an Art Professor at their chief university. There was a series of cartoons by a student. The humour shown was the same as ours, although from the opposite corner of Europe. One was 'The prisoner returns home', He is shown on the station with his luggage, asking 'Where do I get searched?'"

Sent from Campo 78. (Compound 2), 4th June 1942.

"I saw the New Moon on Sunday May 17th about 8.30 I was sitting on the wash-house steps at the time."

Sent from Campo 78. (Compound 2), 11th June 1942.

"One of the batmen brought down a portable gramophone and we had it in our room one evening. The first record was "Solitude" (no joke) sung by Paul Robeson, and the favourite was Alice Fay singing 'Never in a Million Years'. 'The Desert Song' brought back memories (not of the desert, but the film)."[30]

Sent from Campo 78. (Compound 2) 18th June 1942.

"I looked for the New Moon last night but there were too many clouds.

I don't think I've altered very much. Perhaps I'm a bit quieter. My temper is O.K. and I've stopped being sarcastic. Clever remarks come into my head – but I keep them there, which is the best place for them in a prison camp."

Sent from Campo 78. (Compound 2), 3rd September 1942.

"We had a good show on Sunday evening. Each room entered a team of 5 actors. They were given characters to write a play around. – Rich father, his sister, daughter, her sweetheart and a ghost.

---

[30] Gramophone Records could be sent to prisoners in Italy and Germany, through Messrs. H.M.V. Records. They could not be forwarded through the Red Cross.

Sent from Campo 78. (Compound 2), 24th September 1942.

"I had some luck when I went to see our compound play No 3. I was sitting at the end of our crowd, and a sentry, seeing I wore no stripes, turned me out and sent me to the No. 3 supporters. I HAD A TALK WITH BUFF and saw several of the boys.

Last night the orchestra played 'Alexander's Ragtime Band". It brought back memories. I wish we could send photos home, but this is done in Germany only."[31]

Sent from Campo 78. (Compound 2), 29th October 1942.

"So we've had an Income Tax form. Did 'Claude'[32] look happy? I suppose I've got to help to pay my own wages.

The parcel should be here by Xmas. I'm glad you've sent some more shoes. The uppers of these have rotted away.

---

[31] A photograph was sent home from Campo 78 at a later date.

[32] Probably a reference to Claud Schuster Permanent Secretary to the Lord Chancellor's Office at the time. Source: Wikipedia.org. 26.1.16.

I saw the New moon first on Oct 13, a lucky date I hope. The main event of the week is really two events. A hole has been made in the wall so we are able to go into the other compound. All the boys are O.K.

Event number 2 that Fred's compound have put on a play this week "The Middle Watch" by Ian Hay and Stephen King-Hall. This is beyond my powers to describe, all I can say is, it's wonderful. It was in rehearsal for 3 months. They have a whole bungalow for a theatre, the floor luckily being in 3 tiers. The highest is the stage then there are rows of spectators sitting on blankets, then rows on stools placed flat, then on stools upright and finally, on the lowest tier, stools on tables. I was on a blanket. On Sunday I stood outside the window and heard it through again. The next two plays will be Pygmalion and Show Boat. "The girls" had let their hair grow into Eton-crops and had their legs shaved."

Sent from Campo 78. (Compound 2), 5th November 1942.

"I heard on Sunday there was a Lowestoft man among the new prisoners. I found him and he is John Thompson of Carlton Road, next door to Miss Keable. If you should meet his mother, please tell her he is very well. We don't know each other, but he knows Arthur Reynolds and several secondary school boys at the Town Hall. He mentioned Arthur Wright and Mr. Twiddy and the Pigeon Club so I asked if he knew George and Ernie.[33] He knows them well, so I suppose they can remember him. Before joining the Army he was in the Surveyor's office at Bury St. Edmunds and before that was at Beccles. He's about 22. Reg Bailey taught him building at the Tech and he knows about Reg driving to Leicester and back in a day hitting the curb at Worlingham. I can remember Bill Forsyth saying "steady Reg, steady" He was last home in the middle of last year and was captured in June about 100 miles back from where I was captured.

Did you know that a bomb hit Botty's the hairdresser and another hit the shop that used to be Bercham's. Perhaps you were asleep. Is that how the window was broken?"

---

[33] George Sewell and Ernie Sewell were his brothers in law and members of the Pigeon Club.

Sent from Campo 78 (Compound 2), 19th November 1942.

"No mail, so I must write about camp news. I have started to teach French, with a class of six beginners. I've an idea we won't finish the course, but I may have time to give them a rough idea.

On Sunday evening the Salon Orchestra gave a concert. They played selections from The Student Prince, Maid of the Mountains and Show Boat. The choir sang the Lost Cord, Duke Ellington's Blue Indigo, a song by Schumann and Lullaby of Broadway. As usual an excellent show.

On Monday afternoon England played Scotland, quite a gala. We were all allowed down and all the Italian officers were there. England scored the only goal, from a penalty for pushing in the back. Just before the end the Scottish captain was ordered off after a scramble near the English goal. Rough play is definitely not allowed under Italian rules.

At the last meeting of the motor Club a competition was held to choose a Motto. A member of our team had one which I knew was a winner as soon as I heard it –

Ad Adversitatum Superiori – meaning Superior to Adversity. This week we had a medical parcel between four, Allenbury's Food, Bovril, Arrowroot etc."

Sent from Campo 78. (Compound 2), 26th November 1942.

"I've had a Statement of Account from the Paymaster, gross pay still 8/9 a day, less allotment of 5/6, sorry 5/- now, leaving 3/9 to credits. Out of that there's 6½d a week for insurance and 11/1 a month to detaining Power to pay for my 40 lire. The balance is £21-4-5½d which is about what I make it. I've since sent this to you, the statement being dated 1st Sept.

Weather here is cold, with some sunny days. No snow down here, but it will probably stay on the hills until March. I am writing with my feet under the blanket. Did I tell you we have two tier wooden beds now? I'm on top where I can see. It was hard at first after the canvas bed, but I don't notice it now.

Some Red Cross Parcels have come in, and we had a full issue, one each this week. We are praying that the Xmas parcels we hear so much about will get here this year. If they do, and the ordinary ones come in also, we are having them as an extra parcel on Christmas Eve.

My pupils are still keen, in spite of the cold."

Sent from Campo 78. (Compound 2), 30th November 1942.

"Glad to hear news of my old firm. They can manage without me after all, but they've been a long time finishing that contract. Probably shortage of foremen. I often wonder if they'll concentrate on bridge building now.

Sent from Campo 78 (Compound 2), 8th December 1942.

"How did you like "The Gold Rush", I'll be glad to see films again? I expect I'll see a difference in the stars after three years; four in many cases.

The fashions at home will have changed a lot. We hear that men's trousers now have no turn-ups. Under the present rationing, one suit a year is it? I can't see this saving amounting to much. How many turn-ups make one battle dress? By now I suppose most men are in the army too. Still, even if it doesn't amount to much it makes the idle rich realise there's a war on.

Our show, "I have been here before", by J B Priestly is a great success. We have a much bigger mess now. New sergeants have moved into our old mess room and we've taken over a bungalow from the troops. There's plenty of room on the top two stages for mess and classes, a table can form a stage on the third and scenery can be left hanging.

Jock Norval's birthday today. The Lowestoft chap John Thompson had ten letters, his first, last week. Of the new sergeants 11 want to join my French class; that's 15."

Sent from Campo 78. (Compound 2), 17th December 1942.

"My hands are cold. This is the first dull day for over a week, so mustn't grumble I'll enjoy it all the more when I'm at home in front of the fire.

We have read the recent speeches of Churchill and Mussolini and I found them both very interesting. Many forecasts have been made here of the date the war will finish.

Is Lord Haw-Haw still on the radio?"[34]

Sent from Campo 78. (Compound 2), 24th December 1942.

"We are having two Xmas Parcels and one English Ordinary between three men. We in our combine have been lucky. We are drawing three and one between the four of us.

You say the town has altered a lot. Is there a good site for a new Town Hall yet?

The future is very bright and everything in the garden will soon be lovely. I feel sure next year is the year of years."

Sent from Campo 78. (Compound 2), 31st December 1942.

---

[34] William Joyce, aka Lord Haw Haw was a notorious broadcaster of Nazi propaganda to the United Kingdom during World War 11. His announcement 'Germany Calling' was well known. It introduced threats and misinformation broadcast from his base in Hamburg. In 1945, Joyce was captured and returned to Britain, where he was later hanged for treason.

"Your last letter was No. 62. That makes 46 this year, so I've had them all, even though some have taken a long time to come.

There is no comparison between this Xmas and the last two. We had no parcels for the last and on the one before we had just arrived near Alexandria and enjoying bubbly and biscuits."

Sent from Campo 78. (Compound 2), 7th January 1943.

"Christmas Eve was very busy. In the morning I went to the store to carry down parcels. This was quite a big job – a parcel for every man, all to be unpacked and tins opened up. Many hands made light work and after lunch our combine got busy preparing for the day. We iced and decorated the cake made fruit trifles etc. I kept awake to welcome Xmas in, but I seemed to be the only one. We only had one meal in the mess, a huge dinner. I couldn't eat the sweet – rice with currants – so I saved it for next day. The mess was decorated with the coloured paper shavings from the parcels and there was even a Xmas tree with lights. Others were ill on Boxing Day, but Tommo and I are older and have more sense. There was a note in Wilf's letter to say cards are banned, but I still had last year's and I have them set out on my shelf.

New Year's Eve and Day were celebrated in style. Our hosts allowed the dance to keep on until 1am. We made some wine by stewing figs and raisins and adding orange juice and drank 'healths' at midnight. So far the four New Years away from home I have drunk champagne, water, cold Ovaltine and homemade wine.

Tomorrow Jan 6 is Jeep Shaw's 21st birthday and his 846th day as a prisoner. Some score for a youngster."

Sent from Campo 78. (Compound 2), 11th January 1943.

"21 months a prisoner. New moon Jan 8th about 5pm."

Sent from Campo 78. (Compound 2), 14th January 1943.

"On Christmas day and New Year's Day I cleaned my boots with Co-op Polish. Do you remember that pre-war tin I brought away with me? I finished it this Sunday and it was still soft. A good record, after the heat of the desert and the cold of two mountain winters. The boots are an English pair I got two

months ago. They are rather large, which is lucky, as I can wear two pair of socks.

I remember I used to crave for such things as sausage batters. Now it's for something sweet, fruit cake, cream puffs etc. Because with our oil issue we fry our cheese and bread sometimes.

A lorry is going by, cheers outside, now inside, I know what it is – **RED CROSS PARCELS? YES!** And another load reported in sight on the road. Good old Red Cross, our friends for life."

Sent from Campo 78. (Compound 2), 28th January 1943.

"Today is sunny but with a cold wind. This is my washing day and if tomorrow is like this I should get everything dry. The last took over a week.

Fred came in yesterday and didn't seem so bright as usual. He doesn't get on too well with his partner who wants to hoard most of the Red Cross Parcel in the store for a rainy day. I think we've had all our rainy days and so does Fred."

Sent from Campo 78. (Compound 2), 8th February 1943.

"**John Thompson is quite fit, lots of mail but no parcel yet. He hears Arthur Reynolds is at Bury St Edmunds.**"

Sent from Campo 78. (Compound 2), 11th February 1943.

"Weather today has improved, sun shining, although it rained in the night and snow crept down the hills to within a few yards of us.

Do you remember me asking some time ago if you had heard camps were being built for us in the Isle of Wight? The other week I heard of a letter from the War Office confirming this. Last night, however, a letter said the men from this camp were going to Newbury, Berkshire. Of course this may all be duff, but who knows? It passes the time to think about such things. A photographer is gradually working his way round the camp, so I hope soon to send you a snap.

A large load of private parcels have come in. Perhaps a Xmas cigarette parcel for me. There may even be a surprise from our local fund or from the Town Hall. And perhaps

there may not be. I saw the New Moon on Sunday about 5."

Taken Inside Campo 78

The most creased photographs are the best loved.

Sent from Campo 78. (Compound 2), 25th February 1943.

"I had my snap back yesterday, 6 copies, and shall probably send one next week and then one each fortnight. They are very good, and you'll see how well I look."

I can remember things that happened long ago that I had forgotten for years. Changing my seat in the Grand (local cinema) to sit next to you nearly 18 years ago is the oldest of these new memories."

Sent from Campo 78. (Compound 2), 4th March 1943.

"I had over 100 letters in 1942; 47 from you, Windsor Road 31, Uncle Joe and Louise 11, Wilf 5, Leslie 4, Mr. and Mrs. Southgate 3, Mr. Connell, Ralph Denby and Arthur Reynolds 1 each. This year I've had 15 so far, below average.

I went over and had a yarn with John Thompson, He's looking very well; has had plenty of mail, but no parcels yet. He tells me Yarmouth men have had cigarettes from their "Mercury", and that our British Legion is sending some to us. John used to play for Lowestoft Reserves, so will you ask Dad if he can get us news of Town players in the Services.[35]

I still pass my time in the same old way and I have read two good books lately, "Bredon and Sons" the story of a Southwold family, and "Fathers of their People, about a farm near Halesworth."

Sent from Campo 78. (Compound 2), 15th March 1943

"We had snow last Sunday, then the clouds gradually lifted. On Thursday evening about eight they parted a bit to show me the New Moon.

March 6th was Bob's birthday. We saved two cakes from our parcels, each gave half a loaf, mixed it all up and baked it. Then iced it with Klim milk and put Bob 26 on top in chocolate icing.

Several old friends left this camp the other day, they were sorry to go and we miss them after being so long together. We don't know

---

[35] Terry Lynes, the historian at Lowestoft Town Football Club, has confirmed that John Thompson made 11 appearances for Lowestoft Town during the 36-37 season as a mid fielder.

where they've gone, but hope to see them again soon. Clarry Copeland has gone, so he may write to you soon."

Sent from Campo 78. (Compound 2), 18th March 1943

"I've finished lunch and am sitting outside on my stool, with my back against the wall of the next room, and using a Red Cross box as a desk on which to write. The space between the buildings is filled with lines of washing. Bob is reclining at my feet on a blanket, making an attempt to read.

Fred has applied to go before the Repatriation Board. He hasn't looked well for some time and he isn't a young man. So I hope he gets home."

Sent from Campo 78. (Compound 2), 22nd March 1943.

"Two days to my birthday. I'll wish myself Many Happy Returns for you as soon as I wake up. Have you heard from Clarrie yet? Perhaps it is a bit early and perhaps he has lost your address."

Sent from Campo 78 (Compound 2), 30th March 1943.

"The big event of the week was my birthday and the big event of that day was the arrival of your letter of Feb 18th after a blank four weeks.

Another event on my birthday was the announcement on the radio that an exchange of prisoners had been arranged. We've studied the papers very closely but don't know yet the total number that will be exchanged. Of course I'm full of hope, but will take what comes. Clarrie can tell you all about it to date. I had a birthday cake, iced and lettered Cyril Best Wishes 38. Please give all who send me their chocolate ration my very best thanks."

Sent from Campo 78 (Compound 2), 1st April 1943.

"Summer time came in here on the night of Sunday and Monday, but on Monday we had showers all day so couldn't sit outside in the evening.

Our combine had an argument about War Weddings. The "Live Today for Tomorrow We Die" system. I shouldn't have said argument, just a discussion. We never have any heated arguments here. In fact, it's wonderful how good tempered we are, considering we see the same old faces and do the same things day after day. Some men haven't been 100 yards from their beds for nearly two years. I've been on several walks, so have been a mile away at times. A strange thing here is what I call Sunday morning parade. In the morning, from 9 until tea-water at 10 o'clock, a crowd of about 100 men gathers on the roadway between the two rows of bungalows. They stand there and look out over the valley. They don't talk much, just stand and look, although all they can see moving is an odd figure or two on the road or in the fields. They stand like that every morning, but there are about twice as many on Sundays. I haven't got to that stage yet. I can always find something to do."

Sent from Campo 78. (Compound 2), 8th April 1943.

"Today is 6th April, the second anniversary of my capture. Fancy, two years! And not much to show for it except a knowledge of French, and a bit more of costing and photography. I've read a few good books, and above all, found some true friends who have made my life happier. But a prisoner's life can never be much of a life; just because he is still a prisoner. The Church and the Red Cross recognise this and have done their best to make life more bearable. But two years is quite long enough and I am very thankful that news in general is good. The sunshine is a great help to us, and the valley is looking beautiful with its bright green fields and thousands of fruit trees in blossom. I haven't said yet what letters from home mean, but there's no need to. In any case, words can't describe the feeling a letter gives.

The postman has been, and gone. Only two letters for the room."

Sent from Campo 78. (Compound 2), 15th April 1943.

"On the evening of the 6th after I had written, I sat outside on a rock, smoking and thinking about you. About nine o'clock a cloud over the mountain parted and I saw the new moon. Just a thin crescent, only a day or two old.

I can remember the first new moon I saw as a prisoner, on 29th April 1941, when I wondered what would happen before I saw the next. Then things improved, and I saw the next in Italy, on the day we first saw the Red Cross representatives and parcels. I've been reading a book set mostly on the Isle of Capri. I well remember how beautiful the island looked as we sailed by, first steep cliffs rising from the sea, and then when we rounded a corner a green valley dotted with white houses, the sun setting and the sea a wonderful blue. Then Naples, with Vesuvius and its stream of smoke across the sky. I thought of all the places we had seen, Derbyshire, Wales, Walberswick and of how we will soon be seeing them again, with new eyes. O how it will feel to be in the garden again. No more night work at the Hall for me. We've got so much lost time to make up together, my sweetheart. I can imagine how the train home will crawl, and when I see you – well I just can't imagine that; I expect I'll feel terrible."

Sent from Campo 78. (Compound 2), 22nd April 1943.

"I expect the garden is in a mess now, but it will be easy to dig over. We can go over to Daniels nursery at Norwich or the one in Loddon and choose exactly what we want.

I also saw John Thompson the other day. He looks very well now, although he hasn't started football yet."

Sent from Campo 78. (Compound 2), 30th April 1943.

"The weather here is perfect. It must be lovely on those hills under the pines. So near and yet so far. Still we can't have everything."

Sent from Campo 78. (Compound 2), 18th May 1943.

"This has been a very good week. I saw the New Moon last Thursday, heard the first cuckoo, saw the first firefly, and had your Feb 24 letter and the Dec parcel. I was very pleased with everything in the parcel. I shall be able to eat a piece of chocolate in bed for many nights to come. I see you have found out about buying a lb. from the Red Cross. It's a good scheme in these days of rationing.

Now that Clarrie has gone and Jack Eade has taken charge of the officer's mess, I stroll each evening with two other pals. We talk in French only. That French class I started packed in during the cold weather and there isn't much point in restarting now. I'm still a bit slow in speaking French, but can read it alright. I believe we had one or two books at home. Don't throw them away. I shall be able to read to you on dark winter evenings."

Sent from Campo 78. (Compound 2), 27th May 1943.

"When I first met John Thompson I noticed his Suffolk dialect, so you may find I have lost mine. I don't know; but we have been together here for two years so probably speak a Standard English. I know the Scotsmen can be understood now. It's surprising what we find to talk about, but there's never a moment's silence. We talk about the war news or else of what happened before the war. We'll have a shock when we get out and see how the world has changed. Three of us stroll for an hour every evening and do all our talking in French.

Nothing outstanding has happened this week. I forgot the cricket. Each room in this compound and in No 4 has entered two teams in a league. We play in the roadway in each compound, with the proper bats and wickets, but use tennis balls with a strong cover. It's good fun, especially in this compound where the playing area is so small. Two runs if you hit the bottom wall, 4 if it goes over, none if into the top compound behind the wicket, two if into a bungalow and as many as can be run between."

Sent from Campo 78. (Compound 2), 10th June 1943.

"We have heard that Clarrie Copeland died on the way home, but have no details yet. I can hardly believe it. He seemed alright when he left here.

Went to a very good concert the other night, the second show of the Mandliers, an enlarged addition of the Salon Orchestra; six violins, 4 mandolins, 2 guitars, 2 piano accordions, piano, drums and bass with three singers. The programme included selections from the Mikado, the Riff Song, Oh Maiden, My maiden, Volga Boatman, Black Eyes, etc.

Last Saturday's International was postponed for a week because Scotland's goalkeeper, Watson, had a bad smash at pass ball so we played No.3, and lost 5 -3. We tried a new brother at centre-forward, he's supposed to have had a trial with Q.P.R. and he's big enough to be good.

During the winter I took a French class, which packed up when the weather got too cold. Then we didn't restart because we thought we should soon be home. We've decided now to carry on, and tomorrow I'll have 20 pupils which will dwindle to 5 or 6 in a few weeks. I saw the new moon on Saturday, and if my wishes come true and I believe they will, the new class won't last long.

Just heard Clarrie died in Turkey."

Sent from Campo 78. (Compound 2), 17th June 1943.

"It is glorious now, especially in the early morning when the valley is free from heat-haze, and again after dark when the air gets cooler. I usually stroll round the pass ball pitch from eight to ten, come in and make my bed and then sit on the steps of the wash-house for a quarter of an hour. I come in again then, and lie on my bed to wait for the air to cool off before getting in bed. It is so stuffy inside the bungalows.

The new French class seems to be going well, I've given three lessons and still have 18 pupils. Six or eight is plenty for an outside class. I've made a blackboard by blacking a piece of plywood with boot polish. The plywood is the lid off a Canadian parcel case. It's rather fun being a teacher. My pupils sit on the ground with backs to the wall. A long line of hopeful faces. Then I read out a new rule of grammar and four or five faces lose hope. So I explain it all and hope returns, only to fade again at the next rule... The great drawback here is the lack of text-books. I'm using one of Pitman's, costing 1/3^d. If only we had enough for each pupil to have one it would be much easier. Still we manage alright. We are still waiting for the Scottish goalkeeper to get fit so the match last week was North of England v South.

A cricket league has been formed in this Compound for the jeeps, that is, those not good enough for A or B Room Teams. Of course, my team is called Eton, (where the battles are lost) but the others in this room call themselves Harrow. The cads."

Sent from Campo 78. (Compound 2), 21st June 1943.

"How did you enjoy Whitsun? I didn't go far this year, but hope to make up for it quite soon. Just finished 'The End of the Chapter', by John Galsworthy, 956 pages. Started another Zane Grey."

Sent from Campo 78. (Compound 2), 24th June 1943.

"All your letters speak of good news and it does seem as if things are moving at last. Colin read part of his letter aloud last night,

'We are sitting on the lawn in deck-chairs, in lovely weather, drinking iced lemonade and thinking of you'. We all laughed. I wonder why. No wonder new arrivals say we seem strange.

We had a letter from Clarrie's mother. Clarrie died of heart trouble on an Italian hospital ship on March 19th and was buried at Port Said. So, while we were wishing him 'Many Happy Returns', on the 22nd and saying lucky old Clarrie, he was dead. His mother thinks the excitement of going home was too much for him. She is probably right. I'll be excited when I get off that train at Lowestoft.

I'll wait a bit now and see if the postman calls. No sign of him, but hear he has gone down for mail. This has to be handed in now. Dinner is due, so will hold on.

Now, dinner is over mail is in; none for me, one for Bob and two for Tommo. Better luck next time. Colin has just heard his photo got home on 13 May, the day Lowestoft was mentioned in the news."

Sent from Campo 78. (Compound 2), 8th July 1943.

"Some months ago I had great hopes of being home for your birthday. That was not to be. However, whenever that great day is, it's drawing nearer and nearer. I often wonder how long these last four years have seemed to you. It's really under three years since I last saw you but the parting started when the war started. When I look back, the time seems short, especially the last two years. Every day, week and month is much like the last and there is no record of time passing. I haven't had a letter from you lately, and looking at my list, I see the last one came on 30 May, over five weeks ago. Yet it only seems half that time. This slipping away of time is something to be thankful for. I imagine that to you these four years seem like six. Each day flies, because you are so busy, but so much is happening around you all the time that even last Christmas seems a long time ago. But cheer up, Darling, it will all come right one day. I often think of the evenings wasted at the Hall, when I might have been with you. If only I'd known what was coming. But it's rather late for regrets now, isn't it? I was at our gardening class on Sunday evening, and when Ray Newell was talking about outdoor tomatoes, of course I thought of those we used to grow. Then, looking over the valley, I saw the new moon. I wished so hard it's a wonder the moon didn't curl up. Surely this will be the lucky one. What a blessing hope is. There seems to be no mail tonight again."

Sent from Campo 78. (Compound 2), 22nd July 1943.

"We've had some musical instruments sent to the camp and every corner has its learner. Tommo's birthday is on Friday and we are all set to celebrate it with a cake."

Sent from Campo 78. (Compound 2), 28th July 1943.

"I sleep outside now, and it's lovely under the stars. There is never any dew here, perhaps because we are so high, so we don't need any shelter and wake up feeling very fresh and fit. The inmates of a neighbouring room usually sit outside and sing in the evening. The songs may seem old to you, but they are new still to us. They usually start off with "eleven more months and ten more days" and then go on to "beyond the Blue Horizon", "Sleepy Valley", "When Day is Done" etc.

It is now too hot for football so we have packed it up for a while. Cricket is still very popular. It's the best thing that ever came to this camp. There's always plenty of fun in this compound in the early evenings, when the C teams play. There are always missed catches to laugh at, and mighty swipes that always miss the ball. Fortunately, the batsman keeps tight hold of the bat, although the other day one let go and the bat came through the doorway into this room, but hit nobody.

My French class is still going strong. I've had 13 pupils for some time now.

It will be grand to lie on the lawn again. That reminds me of the smell of the grass on the river bank at Southwold. Those were happy days spent nearly on our own doorstep."

Sent from Campo 78. (Compound 2), 6th August 1943.

"I hope you enjoyed yourself at Harold's wedding. It seems the wrong time to get married: no presents about. Or do you give each other coupons instead of presents.

We've had a letter from Bert Winkless. He says whenever he hears someone praising our 8th Army he reminds them of the original members, either dead, wounded or prisoners, who did not have modern arms or overwhelming numbers, but had to do their best in hopeless conditions. I can just imagine him, he looks so inoffensive, but he can hold his own.

Went to the new show last week, "Spring Song for Jennifer," and again last night to a Box Office Night. First show free, second two cigarettes. A musical show written in this camp, and very good, as they all are, but not as good as "Derby Day". Songs from that show are still being sung and whistled."

Derby Day

A Campo 78 Concert Party. Derby Day, an Operetta by A. P. Herbert. The hats were made out of Red Cross Parcels.

Photograph from Cyril's collection.

CAMPO 78 with Monte Morrone in the background

Photographs from Cyril's collection.

117

THE ARMISTICE

In September 1943, the Italian government was nearing collapse. The prisoners of war in Campo 78 heard rumors that the evacuation of the camp was imminent. They woke one morning to find that their guards had deserted. On 14 September, German troops arrived to escort the prisoners northward to captivity in Germany. However, by then, hundreds of them had escaped into the hills.

Cyril was one of those who escaped into the hills. The elation of being free, after so long spent pacing round and round inside the camp, must have been overwhelming. He was free for 13 weeks. He spoke very little about this period after the war but did say he would like to revisit the area again to see people who helped him. Italian people who helped POWs were taking great risks.

In Pietranseri, a town in the Sulmona valley, the town's people were murdered by the Nazis on 21st November 1943 because they were suspected of helping POWs. The German army was particularly harsh on the Italian people after the 1943 Armistice.

Sent from Transit Camp 31979

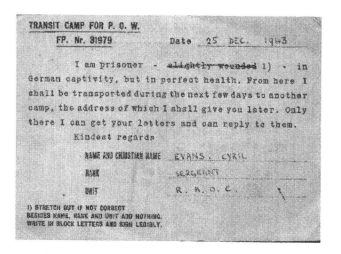

TRANSIT CAMP FOR P. O. W.

FP. Nr. 31979   Date 25 DEC. 1943

     I am prisoner - ~~slightly wounded~~ 1) - in German captivity, but in perfect health. From here I shall be transported during the next few days to another camp, the address of which I shall give you later. Only there I can get your letters and can reply to them.
     Kindest regards

NAME AND CHRISTIAN NAME   EVANS , CYRIL

RANK   SERGEANT

UNIT   R . A . O . C .

1) STRETCH OUT IF NOT CORRECT
BESIDES NAME, RANK AND UNIT ADD NOTHING.
WRITE IN BLOCK LETTERS AND SIGN LEGIBLY.

The above card says Cyril was in German captivity but the transit camp itself may have been in Northern Italy

119

The transferring of prisoners from Italy to Germany was usually done using cattle trucks.

Source: National Ex-Prisoner of War Association website

REDIRECTION OF MAIL

"The International Red Cross Committee at Geneva has undertaken to redirect to the new camp address, as soon as these are known, parcels and correspondence which were addressed to British prisoners of war interned in Italy.

Until the new addresses are known, letters (but not parcels) should continue to be addressed to the last-known camp address in Italy, but in order to reduce the very heavy work of redirection letters sent by a prisoner's family should not in all exceed one a fortnight. Letters may be again sent by air mail, and the prisoner of war air letter cards should preferably be used.

The new camp address in Germany should, of course, be used as soon as they become known. Families may then once again send weekly letters, and also resume sending parcels under the same conditions as for other British prisoners of war in German hands."[36]

---

[36] Source: 'The Prisoner of War', journal, Dec. 1943 page 15.

STALAG V11-A

Stalag VII-A was opened in September 1939 and was Germany's largest prisoner of war camp during World War 2. It lay just north of the town of Moosburg in southern Bavaria, 35 km northeast of Munich, in a flat area surrounded by hills and covered 86 acres. When liberated there were about 80,000 prisoners in the camp. The prisoners were mainly from the North African Campaign taken there from Italian POW camps. Over five and a half years, about 1,000 prisoners died at the camp.

A first hand description of Stalag V11-A, given by Kenneth Rankin after the war.

> "It was a large camp with high wire all round, lookout towers at the corner and guard dogs patrolling the perimeter. The dogs were led on a long leash and woe betide anyone who got in the way.........We were given our gefangenen number and photographed; then we were deloused and all our hair removed."[37]

Sent from Stalag V11-A. 23rd January 1944.

"As you see I've arrived in Germany. My luck was out in Italy. I really thought I should be home for Xmas, right up to the day of

[37] Source: 'Lest we Forget, Fifty Years On', Kenneth Rankin, page 290.

recapture, Still, I've about got over the disappointment now, and I'm smiling again. No permanent address yet, so can't expect letter from you yet. Watch for the New Moon."

Sent from Stalag V11-A. 31st January 1944.

"My 13 weeks of freedom passed very quickly. It is only now as I look back that I realise how long I was free. I always used to tell you to keep smiling, but my own spirits drooped for a time after my recapture, it was a big disappointment; but thousands of us are in the same boat. And I'm O.K. once more now. I've met several friends from Sulmona here, and all seem well. This seems quite a big camp. We are being fitted out with new clothing and have a parcel each week. Weather is like England at this time of year, very dull and wet. I have one photo of you, taken in the back-way of Windsor Road. I have the notecase it was in, a pair of socks knitted by you and my wrist watch, my only links with you."

Sent from Stalag V11-A. 20th February 1944.

"It has snowed every day for a fortnight, so it's time we saw the sun again. I often wonder if you have heard form Jack Norval or Bob Haxton. I shouldn't be surprised to hear they were home. Bill Chaplin is here. You remember I stayed at his house at Ipswich for the night when I was on leave. He left Sulmona about 2 years ago to go to a Working Camp.

Last night we had three chaps in playing music; violin, piano-accordion and guitar. I heard some new songs, "White Cliffs of Dover", "Lovely Week-end" etc. The songs we usually hear are "South of the Border", "Isle of Capri" and "Red Sails in the Sunset", which must seem very ancient to you, if you remember them at all. Another is "Tomorrow is a Lovely Day" which I expect you remember, as we often said so in our letters. But that particular "Tomorrow" seems a long time in coming."

Sent from Stalag V11-A. 6th March 1944.

"I look out at the snow and then imagine being at home sitting in my armchair, you sitting opposite a nice fire burning and the radio turned on. The prisoner's dream of heaven and such dreams bring tears. I am longing to have your first letter. It will be nearly as good as coming home."

Sent from Stalag V11-A. 20th March 1944.

"Another week gone and my birthday nearly here. I don't think I can make a cake this time but we'll have some celebration.

Saw Tommo and several old friends arrive the other day. I've been friendly for several weeks with the Cossey twins from Durban. At one of our previous camps I was in charge of a tent containing South Africans, New Zealanders, French Canadians (who spoke very little English) Yugoslavs (no English) etc. Eric and Wyn Cossey sleep in the next bed. From them I have learnt quite a lot about South Africa, of which they are very proud."

Sent from Stalag V11-A. 27th March 1944.

"Nothing of note this week except the arrival of Tommo, Colin Jacques and the rest of the lads I left behind at Xmas. They all look well except Tommo, who looks very thin. A bad cold has pulled him down. Could not make a cake for the birthday so had raspberries and condensed milk for tea. Should have a good cake for the next."

Sent from Stalag V11-A. 3 April 1944.

"This is Palm Sunday once again and this day three years ago and about this time I was first a prisoner. I am thankful it doesn't seem like three years. It is a lovely spring day here, no clouds and the snow melting. Went to a camp concert last Sunday afternoon. ... The best entertainment in the camp is Hell's Court Broadcasting Station in the next room. They hang blankets across the central passage and from behind it 'broadcast' songs, music, jokes and camp gossip."

Stalag V11-A was visited in April 1944 by the International Red Cross. Below is the official report of that visit which appeared in 'The Prisoner of War', journal, August 1944.

Where conditions called for remedy, the Protecting Power would make representation to the German authorities. When it was reported that food or clothing was required action was taken through the International Red Cross.

OFFICIAL REPORT

STALAG V11-A Moosburg, Germany – visited April 1944.

"There are three sections (1) Officers' Section (2) Other Ranks' Section, (3) Nord Lager (North Camp).

Officers' Section. – The Officers' barrack No. 39 is situated on the eastern end of the camp and is of the same type as the rest of the barracks in the Stalag. The building is separated by barbed wire from the other barracks. The personnel at present total 328 prisoners of war, of whom 162 are British officers, 108 American officers, 10 Indian officers, 21 British and American orderlies, and 27 Italian.

Lighting is unsatisfactory: owing to the arrangement of the electric bulbs on one side of the room only, it is impossible to read or write or work in the other half of the room after dark. The furnishing consists of triple-tier beds in bad repair with paillasses and two blankets per man, some tables and benches.

Bathing and washing facilities are inadequate and all water has to be drawn from a pump in the washhouse, where some wash basins are available. Besides that two taps with drinking water are installed. Laundry has to be done in the washhouse. There is no hot water due to lack of fuel. The clothing position is at present

127

satisfactory. Purchases at the canteen are very limited.

Medical attention for minor cases is given by the British and American medical officers. Serious cases are sent to hospital.

Other Ranks Section. – Barracks no. 5, 6, 7, and 8 form one block and barracks 33, 34, 35 and 36 form a second block. 3,458 British prisoners of war and 52 American prisoners of war are attached to this camp, of whom 1,200 are distributed in seven labour detachments.

Bathing and washing facilities are inadequate. **Food is said to be insufficient and not always well cooked**. There is an adequate supply of trousers and boots. Battle dress blouses, greatcoats, shirts, underwear and towels are much needed. Laundry is done by the men themselves. Only cold water is available. Soap is provided. The canteen is poorly stocked.

Religious services are held by a Church of England padre. Recently the Roman Catholics attended a mass celebrated by a French priest. Plenty of sports kit is provided in the camp, but outdoor recreation is limited by inadequate sports ground. Mail is said to be in order. (Last month letter forms and postcards sent to the various work camps went astray.)

Nord Lager – (North Camp)

All new arrivals pass through this camp for period of quarantine and delousing before entering the transit camp. Accommodation is very primitive. About 400 men were housed in a barracks about 240ft. long and 27ft. wide. They sleep on wood shavings on the floor and are provided with two blankets per man. There is no heating arrangement and no lighting. The windows are small and under the roof. All prisoners received Red Cross parcels on arrival. After delousing the men are admitted in groups of about 50 to the main transit camp. (Visited April, 1944)"[38]

Sent from Stalag V11-A. 10th April 1944.

"Another Easter nearly over, and in spite of being inside the wire, a holiday spirit is in the air. Perhaps the better weather has a lot to do with this.

I have just read "In Search of England", by H. V. Morton and it made me long to be home again. I don't remember if it is too early for primroses, but I can picture that little wood on the corner just through Hulver."

---

[38] Source: 'The Prisoner of War', jounal August 1944 page 12.

Sent from Stalag V11-A. 17th April 1944.

"I've been inside most of the week. Harry and I are making a suitcase from Canadian butter tins, and I hope to arrive home with it.

Harry has had a letter from his wife posted on 3 March and in answer to one he wrote from here in January. So I am looking now for your first letter. What a lot you will have to tell me. A lot must have happened since you last wrote. In August, wasn't it? It seems a terribly long time ago.

During the evenings of this week trial matches have been held to pick a team to play the French on Sunday, that is, tomorrow afternoon. The pitch is just over the wire and we could follow the trials. For the match itself we are being allowed out to the pitch, which looks a good one but very bare at present."

Sent from Stalag V11-A. 15th May 1944.

Gefangenennummer 127463

"As you see, I have a registered number now, so don't forget to put it on letters. I hardly think it worthwhile sending parcels. I've had your letter of 3 March."

Sent from Stalag V11-A. 22nd May 1944.

"Have had no mail since the first. Of course, I would like to have more letters, plenty of them as there are a thousand and one things I want to know.

As the days pass, Saturday, Sunday, Monday, I wonder what we should be doing. Now, about 12 on Sunday in normal time, I would be pottering about in the garden and you cooking dinner, mutton, roast potatoes, etc. I say pottering in the garden because I realise now how little work I used to do. I was thinking yesterday afternoon; you would be out shopping and about four o'clock I would think I was tired, and so go indoors and switch on the radio. I know that whatever work in the garden I had done would be all wasted now, the same as the work in the office. But, when I get home I have an aim, to make the most of every minute. I don't mean work all the while but do only those things that are really worthwhile, as far as I can."

Sent from Stalag V11-A. 12th June 1944.

"The weather must be fine with you now. Everything in the garden should be lovely. The past week has been as usual, so have nothing much to write about. Have seen no plays during the week, but "The Importance of being Earnest", by Oscar Wilde, starts on Tuesday. Am still making that suitcase."

Sent from Stalag V11-A 19th June 1944.

"Last night I was speaking to two Irish Guards from Norfolk and they said I have lost my Suffolk accent. That made me wonder if I have changed much in nearly four years. Living so long with so many accents, we all now speak a sort of Standard English. The hair has gone back on my forehead and got thinner on top. There are lines across my brow, but my mouth looks the same. The corners don't turn down. Arms and legs are thin. I'm sure you'll have no difficulty in recognising me when you see me on the station. In manner, I suppose I'm a bit more serious. I've read through the above and I don't seem to be a very cheerful character, especially as I don't smoke, drink or swear. So you'll have to get busy on me when I get home and put some life into me."

Sent from Stalag V11-A. 26th June 1944.

"Had my second letter on Friday, yours dated 2nd April. Saw the New Moon the same evening as the letter came. Am very glad Bob Thompson got home. I believe he and his pal had a tough time in the mountains all winter."

Sent from Stalag V11-A. 3rd July 1944.

"The South Africans here expect to have leave in England before going home. Eric and Winn Cossy want to see around so can you find out and let them know through me if it is possible to buy and run a second-hand car, motor bike or push bike. They want to plan it all out in advance. Trains are not too convenient."

After the Armistice with Italy Cyril was separated from his fellow POWs in Campo 78. The extract below is part of a letter from Cyril's friends, and former fellow POWs, Fred Dugan and Bill Challis sent from Stalag X1B to, Kathleen, Cyril's wife dated 10th July 1944.

> "You will, of course remember me as I had the pleasure of meeting you at Gillingham. Bill Challis and I are together, the only two of the old unit, as we were separated from Buff, Clewlow, Elmy Turton, Geast and Muir at another camp in Germany. Bill and I are keen to know what

happened to Cyril. Did he get home? We all made a bid for freedom in Italy, but our present hosts had different ideas. We were treated very well and after three weeks in our old camp in Italy with plenty of pleasing things for our tummies, we were sent to Germany by sail. Some of us (including myself) were sent to working camps. Bill Challis works for a firm here but I have an office job in camp. Percy Parker, Gell and Carlisle are in Germany, they left Italy before us. Tell Cyril that Busty Perks and many others got home. We left Messes Dover; Amos also Salmon Syd at our last camp. I had to part with my nephew there too, as he is an N.C.O."

Sent from Stalag V11-A. 31st July 1944.

"I had quite a good time on your birthday and hope you did also. It was impossible to make a cake so I made up a very nice trifle. I put raspberries in syrup over broken biscuits and let it soak all afternoon.

I've been told to wish you Many Happy Returns by several friends here. After tea I went round to see Harry and pay off a little bet and then watched England beat Scotland 3 – 1.

Saw the New Moon. Saw a variety show by our "official" concert party, the "Captivators". Wonder what our talkies are

like now; Deanna Durbin and Judy Garland must be quite grown up."

Sent from Stalag V11-A. 14th August 1944.

"Another week nearer the great day. Quite a lot of mail has been coming in. We've had news of three more old friends arriving home. Have been reading "Your mind and How to Use it", No, not where to find it."

Sent from Stalag V11-A. 21st August 1944.

"After the war the Red Cross are publishing a book on all aspects of P.O.W. Life. Price £3-3-0 all profits to Red Cross. I've put my name down for a copy. And ran into a discussion with Colin Jacques, with whom I share "brews". He's quite willing to give the money but wants no reminders of this life in his house after the war. I say we can never forget it so why not have the book as well. I often think of my good friends in the Sulmona Valley and hope to be able to see them again.

Have been busy this week putting all my old notes into a notebook i.e. note of Roses, Costing, House Plans etc. We really must grow roses after the war. When I open my notebook I can smell them. Went to see "Mourning Becomes Electra" by Eugene O'Neill and enjoyed it very much, although a tragedy."

Sent from Stalag V11-A. 4th September 1944.

"I'm sitting on top of the world just now because I've had another letter from you, your third. The great thing is it's dated 3 Aug. It is wonderful darling to touch something that you have touched only a few weeks ago. It seems to bring us very near to each other. I feel sure we shall soon really be together once more."

Sent from Stalag V11-A. 11th September 1944.

"Everything is going in its same sweet way. Saw the show "The Duke in Darkness" the other evening and it's quite up to the usual BWB standard, although the subject, the story of a duke imprisoned for 15 years is getting rather near home. The official party "The Captivators", are giving a band-show so I shall be going out for the evening again."

It was reported in the 'Prisoner of War' journal that there were 24 members of the band in Stalag V11-A. The music library had 62 pieces and was steadily growing. New music was bought out of the proceeds of the collections taken at the weekly concerts.[39]

Sent from Stalag V11-A. 18th September 1944.

"I have been speaking to a chap who early last year was at Kessingland Beach Holiday Camp. He was there some time and was often in Lowestoft, Yarmouth and Norwich. The Odeon he says, looks like part of the front line, and I had quite a job to explain where the Marina was – and I mean was, as I hear the whole block is open. Quite a good site for a new town hall – or perhaps there is a more convenient one further south, which seems to be the direction in which the town will spread.

There was a boxing tournament yesterday, but I didn't go. I saw the last one and was not very thrilled. Football is still very poplar and our Section team "Agitators" are in the final of the room cup. I think they'll win, and top the league also. I had a game the other day a scratch match, 15 minutes each way and I was terribly out of breath. The

---

[39] Source: 'The Prisoner of War', journal Sept 1942 page 7.

remarkable thing was, I scored both our goals and more remarkable still with my left foot."

Sent from Stalag V11-A. 25th September 1944.

"I'm lucky again. I had your 11 Aug letter last Monday. That makes four from you. It's good to get these recent letters; they bring you so much nearer. I was in France five years ago. Five years! It's a lifetime for a chicken."

Sent from Stalag V11-A 2nd October 1944.

You say you had a dream in which we met as strangers. That's strange I've been thinking on the same lines and believe I have said so in a letter. We may seem like strangers, but only on the surface. We've been living such different lives. You have been on your own, working quite successfully, making a good ending out of a bad beginning; managing all our affairs, seeing after rent and rates, taking responsibilities. My life has gone in the opposite direction. For the past three years at least I have had no responsibilities of any kind: just one of a crowd, drifting along a narrow stream with never-changing scenery. Your world to you seems quite normal. I shall be lost in it for a while. As you say it will be like being married again and starting life anew."

Sent from Stalag V11-A. 23rd October 1944.

"The New Moon on Friday said "keep hoping" Better times will come. The Red Cross says men abroad for three years won't pay Income Tax. Full particulars at local Office. The letter was read to us, and was hard to follow, but it seems that a wife's salary can be taxed separately, if preferred. The Town Hall or Income Tax Office will explain.

Ralph Thompson's mother writes that she has seen Bob Haxton and Jock Norval. I sent a card to Bob's father some time ago. We have often wondered about them, think that they were in Germany. Several others have been lucky and arrived home. In fact, some have been home and now rejoined us again. They must like P.O.W. Life. They tell us that pay has increased; about 2/6 a day I believe so check up on that Income Tax.

Saw "Barretts of Wimpole Street" with one of the Sulmona stars as Elizabeth Barrett. Very good, but rather grim for this life. The BWB are putting on this week "To Have the Honour" by A A Milne which should suit us very well. Going to Classical Concert this afternoon (Sunday)."

Sent from Stalag V11-A. 6th November 1944.

"Another Sunday here and another month already a fifth over. I, with many others, go to church at ten. The church is packed, both for our service and the R.C. I look forward to these services the sermons always give me something to think about. And I seem to have plenty of time for thinking. I often read favourite passages, Psalms 23, 121 and 143 and first Corinthians 13. I just feel that the wonderful writing in these (and also in two or three books I have read) does me good. It gives me patience; and we certainly need patience now. All of us."

Sent from Stalag V11-A. 13th November 1944.

"I have found books to be a very great friend, in fact, life would be hard without them. I've made a list of those I'd like to buy when I get home. About twenty in all, all the way from "Gone with the Wind" to "Fundamentals of Health.""

Sent from Stalag V11-A. 20th November 1944.

"I thought it about time for the New Moon, so after tea tonight I went for a stroll. The sun had set and the sky was slightly hazy. I walked up and down while it became darker and just before six o'clock I saw a glow, which brightened, and there was the New Moon. I felt quite bucked seeing it like this and I wished hard it brings all we have been hoping for, for so long. I am writing this on Saturday evening and when I looked outside just now I saw in the east the three stars of Orion's Belt, for the first time. Ralph Thompson calls them the Gisborough Stars because he and his Kathleen used to watch them there before he came abroad.

I was eating chocolate as I strolled, and this is why. On Monday the 13th I had a Sulmona parcel, posted 9 June 1943. In case you have forgotten, it contained pyjamas, towel, socks, dentifrice and brush, etc. and 3 ½ lbs. chocolate. It was certainly a big surprise.

Ralph had a letter from Jock Norval. He and Bob got through alright as you have heard."

Sent from Stalag V11-A. 4th December 1944.

"December the last month of a year of hope and disappointment. Roll on 1945! I'll be thinking of you at Xmas and New Year. Have a good time and look to the future, which we know will be bright. When I get out of the army we will be free – to stay at 'Kathrill' and lay out the garden and decorate the house exactly as we want it – build on a new site (but I don't know a better in Lowestoft), or get a job in say Surrey, Sussex or Kent, and start afresh in very lovely country."

Sent from Stalag V11-A. 11th December 1944.

"Every evening now I talk and read with a chap who lives just outside Paris so my French should improve quite a bit. He is learning English so we help each other and pass the evenings very nicely."

Sent from Stalag V11-A. 18th December 1944.

"I've had my French lesson, and really feel I'm getting somewhere. My friend first read something so that I can get the rhythm, then from his grammar he reads English and I read the French and we finish by talking about various things, home cooking etc. I believe you could learn the language quicker than I as you have a better ear. I remember *you* know most radio personalities by their voice, which I couldn't, except of course Stainless Stephen and Mr. Middleton. Do you remember "The Vagabond Lover?" No I don't mean me, although a year ago this past week, when I was recaptured, I certainly looked the part. Our main concern now is, will Xmas parcels arrive in time?"

Sent from Stalag V11-A. 25th December 1944.

"Very Merry Christmas. Xmas Eve and all in the best of spirits here. Am sure this will be the best I have had for the past few years. We have been busy decorating the room with streamers and trees and it looks good, even if the main colour is white."

Sent from Stalag V11-A. 1st January 1945.

"I had a very good Xmas. We had some music in the room that evening, which brightened up after a slow beginning. With the church service nearly all carols and then a musical evening, my voice had plenty of exercise. Perhaps you didn't know I had one. I should have started this letter by saying "Thank you for the presents" because when I went to bed on Xmas morning I acted the part of Santa Claus for you and put on my shelf the pyjamas and socks from your Italian parcel and in my sack the tooth brush, handkerchief etc. So you see Christmas comes in spite of all our troubles and we can truly say 'Hark, the Herald Angels Sing'."

Sent from Stalag V11-A. 22nd January 1945. (1)

"I see in one of your letters that we would not be able to buy a car yet because they will be dear. You are right! I've been figuring it out like this – tax £10, insurance £8, drop in value £10. That's nearly £30 a year and over 10/- a week. Petrol for just normal runs, to and from work, out on Sunday, one or two evenings, and to see the "city" will add up to more than 10/- a week. Say £60 a year. Now, a summer cruise costs £1 a day, that's £30 a fortnight for two. Rail fare to Norwich for two for every match only £6 fare to any part of England at most £10 for two. Two good cycles about £15. Rail touring tickets 10/- each, no, we won't have a car until motoring gets much cheaper. I promised the good people of Sulmona we would visit them after the war. We shall probably fly to Rome before many years are past."

Sent from Stalag V11-A. 22nd January 1945. (2)

"I think it advisable to day-dream as much as possible about better days, to read good books, to study a little. Anything rather than mope around sinking lower and lower into misery and hopelessness. I hope I haven't painted too black a picture of prison life but the danger of boredom is so plain to see. I think over and over again incidents in our past life. And always some little thing comes back. Even when writing this I think of the geese on the common near Whissonsett, the smell of the billiard room there. Such little pictures and memories are continually flashing into my mind. I saw the New Moon Tuesday and wished as hard as ever, in spite of disappointment."

Stalag V11-A

Potato-peeling at Stalag VIIA.

Source: The 'Prisoner of War' journal June 1943 page 9

The Prisoner of War journal September, 1944.

Prisoner of War Post

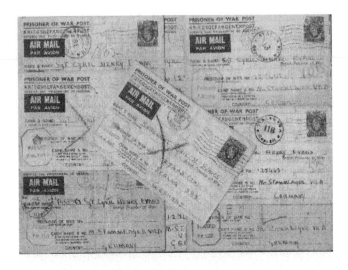

Red Cross Parcel Receipts

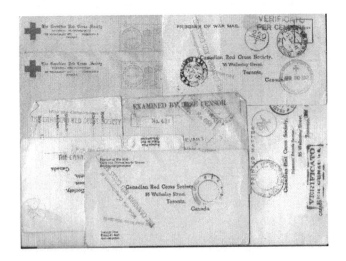

STALAG 383

Stalag 383, Hohenfels, Bavaria, Germany.
(formerly Oflag, 111C).

The address the letters were sent from changed at this point, to Stalag 383. I haven't found any reference to the reason for this from the letters. However, it is likely to have been due to the overcrowding in Stalag V11-A by the end of 1944. As the allies became more successful and the war drew to a close, the Germans were finding it more and more difficult to feed the POWs.

> "One of the cruel ironies for a POW is that his own side' gains and victories often expose him to danger or bring about a dramatic worsening of his living conditions."[40]

Sent from Gefangenennummer 127463 STALAG 383. 12th February 1945.

"As you can see by the address I've arrived at a new camp. I've already made some good friends and start attending a Photography class tonight. Don't know about French, as just now we are rather busy during the daytime getting settled in."

---

[40] Source: 'For You The War Is Over' Page 45, H Buckledee 1994. Don Fraser Print, Sudbury Suffolk.

Sent from Stalag 383. 19th February 1945.

"Another Sunday here and the start of yet another week. Saw a lovely sight the other evening, the New Moon with Venus quite near it. Surely a sign for the future. I pray that it is and that we shall soon be together again. It will soon be my birthday. What a long time we have been parted!"

Sent from Stalag 383. 19th March 1945.

"Well, my birthday week is here once again I've had high hopes of something extra good this time, but it is not to be. Trying a new dish for supper as this is Sunday, oats and dried egg mixed with layer of bacon in the centre."

The Importance of Being Earnest, Stalag 383

Source: National Ex-Prisoner of War Association website.

LIBERATION

Stalag VII-A was liberated on 29th April 1945. The camp's 240 guards surrendered. At the time of liberation there were 76,248 (7,975 British) prisoners in the camp.

Stalag 383 was liberated on 22nd April 1945, by US forces.

Liberation had been a long time coming. Cyril arrived back in the United Kingdom on 14th May 1945 and proceeded to the Dispersal Centre on 23 July 1945.

Stalag 383 Liberation April 1945.

Source: National Ex-Prisoner of War Association website

AT LAST

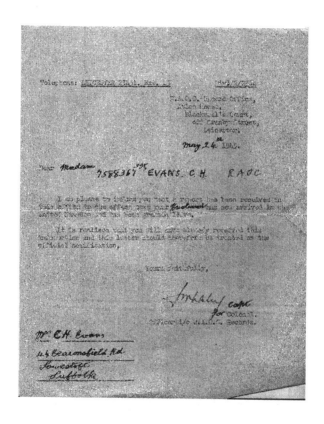

THE RETURNED PRISONER

One of the main problems for returned prisoners was adjusting to a normal diet. The leaflet below was provided by the War Organisation of the Red Cross to help with this

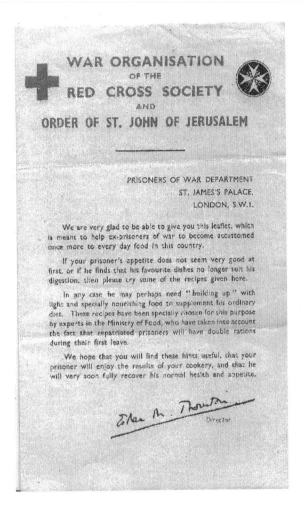

WAR ORGANISATION
OF THE
RED CROSS SOCIETY
AND
ORDER OF ST. JOHN OF JERUSALEM

PRISONERS OF WAR DEPARTMENT
ST. JAMES'S PALACE,
LONDON, S.W.1.

We are very glad to be able to give you this leaflet, which is meant to help ex-prisoners of war to become accustomed once more to every day food in this country.

If your prisoner's appetite does not seem very good at first, or if he finds that his favourite dishes no longer suit his digestion, then please try some of the recipes given here.

In any case he may perhaps need "building up" with light and specially nourishing food to supplement his ordinary diet. These recipes have been specially chosen for this purpose by experts in the Ministry of Food, who have taken into account the fact that repatriated prisoners will have double rations during their first leave.

We hope that you will find these hints useful, that your prisoner will enjoy the results of your cookery, and that he will very soon fully recover his normal health and appetite.

Eileen M. Thornton
Director

Recipe pages

AFTERWORD

Cyril's letters contained no sign of hatred, no bravado and hardly any mention of the Italian or German guards. The melancholy rarely showed through.

Accounts written after the war by ex POWs tell of a harsher reality than was put forward at the time through letters home. The emphasis at the time, was to keep morale up, not to let the enemy know you were down, and not to risk worrying friends and relatives at home. After the war this incentive was gone and accounts telling of the harsh conditions were published.

A request being played for a POW on Vatican Radio seems like an incredibly civilised thing to happen amid war. It must have taken a fair bit of organisation to gather requests from prisoners.

Nothing is known about the 13 weeks Cyril spent at liberty in Italy but the following excerpt from the letter sent from Stalag V11-A. 22nd January 1944 (1). Suggests he was helped by Italian civilians.

> **"I promised the good people of Sulmona we would visit them after the war. We shall probably fly to Rome before many years are past."**

Cyril brought home with him a copy of 'Lend Me Your Ears, An Anthology of Shakespearean Quotations, Familiar, and Not-So-Familiar, selected by Reyner Barton, which carries on the inside front and back covers, the Stalag 383 stamp.

Four letters sent after the war in 1945, to Cyril from fellow POWs, have survived. They are from Fred Dugan, Bob Haxton, Bob Thompson and Colin Jacques. He kept in touch with Fred Dugan for many years and attended several Prisoner of War reunions in London.

Cyril returned to the Borough Engineers Department at Lowestoft Borough Council after the war. He and Kathleen returned to live in Walmer Road, Pakefield. and he went on to live a full and happy life, as the football match ticket below shows.

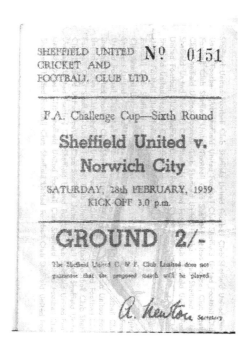

Cyril died in 1962.

The title page of Lend Me Your Ears, a book Cyril brought back home with him from Stalag 383.

The inside cover showing the Stalag 383 stamp

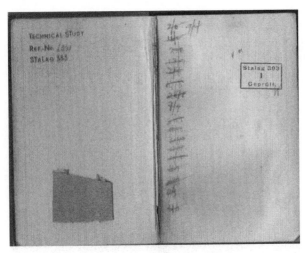

KRIEGIE PLEDGE

I think that I shall never see
A meal that won't appeal to me!
Admitted that in days gone by
I've left a crumb of apple pie
Or a tiny scrap of meat
On my plate I didn't eat!
But now it is my firm resolve
To make all food that's near dissolve
That any dumb and wasteful fool
Might leave around to make me drool!
And I'll never hesitate
To clean the scraps all off my plate!
Meals are missed by fools like me,
But never again – I guarantee!

Author Unknown

BIBLIOGRAPHY

Buckledee, H, "For You The War Is Over," page 45, 1994 Don Fraser Print, Sudbury Suffolk

Doyle, Peter, "Prisoner of War In Germany," page 17 Shire Publications Ltd 2011.

Harris G H, 'Prisoner of War and Fugitive', (Gale & Poldon: Aldershot, 1947).

National Archives - Research carried out by Tom Tulloch-Marshall website www.TomTulloch-Marshall.co.uk

Prisoner of War - leaflet published on behalf of The War Organisation of the British Red Cross January 1942.

Rankin, Kenneth, "Lest We Forget, Fifty Years On,"page 290, Kenneth Rankin, 23 Archery Fields, Odiham, Hants., England. 1989.

The Heritage Centre, Wildes Score, Lowestoft.

The Prisoner of War – The official Journal of the Prisoners of War Department of the Red Cross and St. John War Organisation, St, James's Palace, London. SW1
        Vol 1. No.5 – September 1942
        Vol 2. No.14 – June 1943
        Vol 2. No.15 – July 1943
        Vol 2. No.20 – December 1943
        Vol.2. No.21 – January, 1944
        Vol.3. No.29 – September 1944

The War Diaries of the HQ 3rd Armoured Brigade and the Brigade Ordnance Field Park with the permission of the National Archives.

Tudor, Malcolm, "British Prisoners of war in Italy: Paths to Freedom, page 13, 14 and 15, Emilia Publishing, Woodlands, Bryn Gardens, Newtown, Powys, SY16 2 DR. 2000.

Ward, Edward, "Give me Air", page 46. John Lane The Bodley Head London, 1946,

WEBSITES:
www.tankmuseum.org. – 29.12.15.
Wikipedia.org/wiki/red_cross_parcel 16.1.2016
www.oldlowestoft.co.uk 15.2.2016
www. Prisonerofwar.org.uk

The poem, 'Kriegie Thoughts' - Author Unknown and the poem, Kriegie Pledge – Author Unknown. Every effort has been made to find the author of these poems, if anyone knows please let me know.

Permission has been sought wherever possible to reproduce the images contained in this book. Where I have not yet succeeded I would be happy to include full acknowledgment.

Index of POWs Mentioned in Letters

Stapley, Buff (Arthur)	Campo 78
Stevens, Bob	Campo 78
Thompson, Bob	Campo 78
Thompson, John	Compo 78
Thompson Ralph	Stalag V11-A
Thurton, Les	Stalag V11-A
Winkles, Bert	Campo 78

Dear Reader

If you have enjoyed reading this book,
then please leave a review on Amazon.
Thank you.

About the Author

Sandra Delf has always been interested in history. She is a volunteer at Lowestoft Museum and belongs to a U3A Family History group. It wasn't until she retired that she read these letters, written by her father, from prisoner of war camps, and was inspired to write this book.

She can be contacted at the website below and would be pleased to hear from anyone who has known anyone mentioned in this book or was in Campo 78, Stalag V11-A or Stalag 383.

https://www.facebook.com/Sandra-Delf-881404858618606/?fref=ts

Printed in Poland
by Amazon Fulfillment
Poland Sp. z o.o., Wrocław

55092311R00094